Navigable Waterways

Companion volume in this series:

Roads and Vehicles by Anthony Bird

L. T. C. Rolt

Navigable Waterways

The *Industrial Archaeology* series
edited by L. T. C. Rolt

ARROW BOOKS

ARROW BOOKS LTD

3 Fitzroy Square, London W.1

AN IMPRINT OF THE HUTCHINSON GROUP

London Melbourne Sydney Auckland
Wellington Johannesburg Cape Town
and agencies throughout the world

First published by Longmans 1969
Arrow edition 1973

Made and printed in Great Britain
by C. Nicholls & Company Ltd
The Philips Park Press Manchester M11 4AU

ISBN 0 09 907800 7

Contents

List of Illustrations

Illustration Acknowledgements

The thanks of the author and publisher are due to the following who supplied
illustrations: The British Waterways Board for Nos 5, 7, 18, 25, 26, 28, 32,
34. Mr Ronald Barker for No 13. Mr Eric de Maré for Nos 12, 14. Oscar and
Peter Johnson, Ltd, Lowndes Square Gallery for No. 2. Mrs Angela Rolt for
Nos 6, 8. Mrs Sonia Rolt for No. 16. Mr R. W. Shopland for No. 11.
Professor A. W. Skempton for No. 4. Mr Rex Wailes for Nos 15, 19, 20.
Mr George Watkins for No. 33. Mr C. J. Weaving for Nos 21, 22. Nos 1, 3,
9, 10, 17, 23, 24, 27, 29, 30, 31 are from the author's collection.

Thanks are also due to Professor Skempton for his permission to reproduce
the maps which illustrate the first two chapters; also the drawing of John
Smeaton's lock. These were originally prepared for his Paper to the Newcomen Society.

Introduction

The British inland waterway system, consisting partly of navigable rivers and partly of still canals, combines beauty with utility to a unique degree. Hard-headed 'Companies of Proprietors' improved rivers or dug canals for strictly commercial motives, for waterways were then as important to the national economy as motorways are today. Yet at the same time these men made a major contribution to the beauty of the English landscape. No other product of the industrial revolution has contributed so much. To some extent this was fortuitous, because a highway whose surface is a mirror of water finds a place in the landscape much more easily and naturally than do later roads of steel or tarmacadam. Yet all the man-made works associated with waterways, the locks and bridges, the warehouses and lock cottages, no matter whether they be simple and functional or self-consciously architectural in design, reveal that the waterway engineers, no less than the contemporary architects of country houses, were concerned that their work should make a positive contribution to the English scene. True that age has now mellowed them, yet there is a sense of fitness about them which proclaims that, even when they were new, they could never have done violence to their surroundings.

When our waterways were built, the engineering profession in this country was in its infancy. Indeed, in building our waterway system, British civil engineers cut their wisdom teeth; they began the work as mere tradesmen, they finished it as professionals. Building waterways was the 'prentice work of men who later built the railways and who are now building motorways. The periods of canal, railway and road construction overlap so that a continuous thread of accumulating knowledge and experience unites all three.

At a time when unfinished and projected motorways represent a chapter in this long story that is still being written, it is instructive and salutary to clamber down on to the waterway towpath and read the chapter with which the story opened. When the Institution of Civil Engineers was founded in 1828—mainly by canal engineers, and with the most distinguished of them all as President in the person of Thomas Telford—it was necessary to define the role of a professional engineer for the purpose of obtaining a Royal Charter. Thomas Tread-gold supplied the definition. It was, he said, 'the art of directing the great sources of power in nature for the use and benefit of man'. True enough, but the contrast between an eighteenth-century canal and a twentieth-century motorway prompts some uneasy reflections upon the course which the engineer's art has taken. It is so great as to pose the question whether the attitude of man towards nature has not undergone a fundamental change. As knowledge has vastly increased man's borrowed powers, so his attitude towards the source of those powers, has subtly altered. Whereas once he was concerned with art to direct, now he presumes with strength to command. What began as a sensitive and loving partnership has ended in a brutal and arrogant rape. In justifying such conduct, the argument of expediency has so far prevailed because, to the shortsighted, its logic appears unassailable. But man cannot live by bread alone and it is to be questioned whether his 'use and convenience' are best served in the long term by turning what was once a great landscape garden into a man-made wilderness which is not even designed upon a human scale but to a measure determined by machines.

Such are the reflections which these placid, man-directed waters prompt and in this respect it is a good thing that their beauties are now far more widely appreciated than they used to be even so recently as twenty years ago. Until the end of the last war, those responsible for maintaining our waterways and those who worked the dwindling commercial traffic over them lived in a forgotten world, existing unsuspected in our midst. We could not fail to be aware of great rivers such as Thames, Severn or Trent, but the canals which comprise the greater part of the waterway system we simply did not *see* at all. Like homely, too familiar faces or constantly chiming clocks, we took them so much for granted that they no longer made any impact on our consciousness. We might cross over them a thousand times in the course of hurried journeys by rail or road without ever questioning where they came from, where they were going to, or who built them and when. Occasionally some rare visitor from the outside world ventured to explore them, a William Bliss, a Temple Thurston, a Bonthron or a

Neal, and would subsequently describe his experience in print rather
as one returning from Arabia Deserta. But these writings—unde-
servedly in some cases—made little impact.

Today, all that is changed. We have rediscovered our waterways
and, paradoxically, this rediscovery has coincided with the death of the
old indigenous and colourful commercial life of the canals. Whether a
modern fibreglass cruiser is a worthy substitute for a commercial
'narrow boat' in all the brave splendour of bright paint and polished
brass work, or whether a yacht marina is an appropriate end' for an
eighteenth-century range of canal warehouses may be questioned.
Those who deplore such changes must take consolation in the fact that
at least they are positive and spell new life of a kind. The only alternative was a weed-choked and ruinous death.

This new role of Britain's waterways as a holiday amenity instead
of a commercial necessity means that more and more people are
seeing and appreciating the greatest single monument we have of
pre-railway age engineering. By their works you shall know them and,
as I have earlier indicated, such an intimate acquaintance with the work
of our first great engineers cannot fail to be salutary.

Everything that man has made has a voice. Every earth bank, every
wall of baked brick or cut stone, every iron beam speaks of the men who
made them, telling us much, not only about the secrets of their technique
but about the thought and the aspiration which led them to apply that
technique in the way they did. By the marks that our ancestors have left
upon the natural world, by the art with which they sought to direct
nature for their use and convenience we may judge their view of the
world, a mysterious world, a world of which we now have so much more
knowledge and so much less respect. This is the most salutary lesson of all.

But before we can read this language we need knowledge and
mental discipline to steer a right course between the opposite poles of
the two cardinal errors that can sway our judgment: the error of hind-
sight which, by the application of our own standards to the work of the
past, leads to contempt; the romantic error which regards the past as
a golden age and looks upon all its works with uncritical admiration. It
is this knowledge and discipline which enables a trained archaeologist
to determine the provenance of a fragment of pottery or bronze
ornament which is meaningless to us. It is the purpose of industrial
archaeology to apply the same technique to the artifacts of our industrial revolution.

A thorough knowledge of the social, economic and political history of the culture he has chosen to study is an essential part of the archaeologist's equipment, for it helps him to weigh the significance of his findings in the field. But there is a constant cross-fertilization here, for his findings help to enlarge and illuminate this background of knowledge. Indeed if the period he is studying is very remote, knowledge of it may largely have been built up from the evidence of past finds. In the case of a period so recent as the industrial revolution of the eighteenth and early nineteenth centuries this is obviously not so, but we should be wrong to assume from the abundance of written records that they can provide us with all that can be known about it. The material progress of mankind does not proceed at an even rate. After centuries of slow growth, the industrial revolution brought about an acceleration as hectic as it was unique in history. It was a current without precedent in human affairs in which many important aspects of human activity were swept into a forgotten limbo in little more than the span of a generation. We are wrong to assume, therefore, that we know all that is to be known about the recent past simply because it is so recent and because it has left us an abundance of written records. We need to supplement these records with knowledge gained by archaeological field work, in other words by a close study of the artifacts of the period.

Britain's inland waterways are a good case in point. Objects of wonder at the time they were built, they fell into neglected obscurity as the pace of industrial revolution quickened. They were at once too old to attract eyes hypnotized by the changes wrought by steam power and the internal combustion engine and too recent in origin to claim the attention of orthodox archaeologists. Consequently, until twenty years ago, it was true to say that we knew more about our Roman roads than we did about our waterways. Not only was this ignorence due to lack of exploration of the waterways themselves but to a failure to study their written records.

Today, however, the thousands of people who are exploring our waterways with fresh eyes need not lack the necessary background knowledge as to their social, economic and political history; who built them and to what end; their profitability and what social purpose they once served. For when the waterways came under the aegis of the British Transport Commission, all the records of the old canal companies that had lain so long forgotten were gathered together in one place, indexed and made available for study. A number of writers have availed themselves of this opportunity, most notably Charles Hadfield whose series of regional canal histories (see Bibliography) provides the waterway explorer with the essential background of historical knowledge. These books supply the when, the where and the wherefore of the waterways. They will tell you the names, some famous, some unknown, of the engineers who planned and built each waterway, but they cannot tell you what men they were or how they set about their work and tackled their technical problems. For this is knowledge that no written records can disclose. Only brick and masonry work, oak and iron can tell that side of the story. The printed word cannot hope to match their solid three-dimensional eloquence. But it can tell you where and how to look and that is the purpose of this book. It is by no means a complete study; there is much more to be learned.

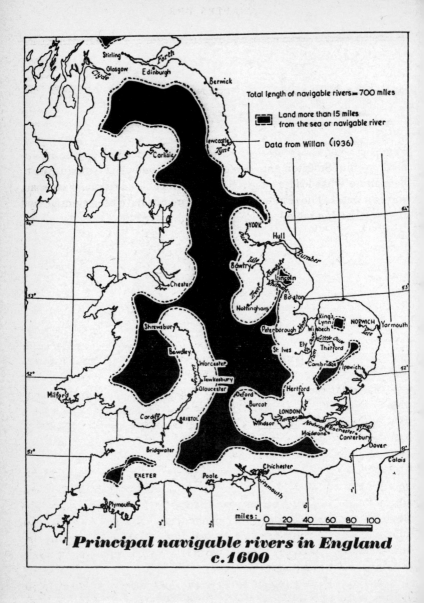

Total length of navigable rivers = 700 miles

Land more than 15 miles from the sea or navigable river

Data from Willan (1936)

Stirling
Glasgow
Edinburgh
Forth
Clyde
Berwick
Newcastle
Tyne
Carlisle
YORK
Hull
Ouse
Humber
Chester
Bowtry
Idle
Trent
Foss Dyke
Witham
Lincoln
Boston
Nottingham
King's Lynn
Wisbech
NORWICH
Yarmouth
Yare
Shrewsbury
Peterborough
St. Ives
Ely
Little Ouse
Thetford
Cambridge
Ipswich
Bewdley
Worcester
Severn
Tewkesbury
Gloucester
Milford
Oxford
Burcot
Hertford
Cardiff
BRISTOL
Windsor
LONDON
Thames
Medway
Rochester
Maidstone
Canterbury
Dover
Calais
Bridgwater
EXETER
Poole
Chichester
Portsmouth
Plymouth

miles: 0 20 40 60 80 100

Principal navigable rivers in England c.1600

CHAPTER ONE

River Improvement before 1700

When the canal age was at its height, a number of engineers, including John Smeaton and Thomas Telford, conducted experiments to determine what load a single horse was capable of drawing on road, rail and water. The results of these experiments have been summarized in the following table.[1]

	tons
Average pack-horse load	$\frac{1}{8}$
Stage waggon, soft road	$\frac{5}{8}$
Stage waggon, macadam road	2
Barge on river	30
Barge on canal	50
Wagon on iron rails	8

It was characteristic of the new, inquiring spirit that was abroad in the canal age that a comparison between the different forms of transport should have been made in such exact terms. For although the overwhelming advantage of water transport had been apparent since the Middle Ages it had never before been expressed in figures. It was an advantage which would justify an ever increasing expediture of capital as trade expanded, first on the improvement of rivers for navigation and later on the construction of still canals.

In the Dark Ages and until Saxon times inland navigation was much more extensive than it subsequently became. River channels were unobstructed, allowing tides to sweep far inland. These tides not only kept river channels scoured but enabled boats to travel with them to inland wharves well beyond the tidal limit. This was because the incoming tide caused the fresh water in the river to 'back up', in other words the tidal water acted as a dam.

The River Severn offers perhaps the best surviving example in Britain of this far-reaching effect of tidal influence. The 'Kings high stream of Severn' was a 'free river' throughout the Middle Ages, no private interests being permitted to obstruct it, with the effect that the powerful tides of the Bristol Channel enabled boats to penetrate far inland. Naturally such navigation was dependent on the vagaries of tides and fresh water flow, but it was not until 1858 that, under heavy pressure from interested canal companies, the present locks were completed and navigation became more regular. But despite the presence of locks and weirs at Llanthony (Gloucester) and Lower Lode (Tewkesbury), high spring tides still flow inland as far as Upton on Severn and back up the fresh water 1 ft at the tail of Diglis Locks, Worcester, seventy-eight miles from the sea at Avonmouth. This backing up at Diglis occurs 5 hrs 10 min after high water at Avonmouth.[2]

We may gather from this some idea of the advantage of tides to the ancient inland navigators. They may have made water transport possible only at certain times and seasons, but in a country largely devoid of metalled roads this limitation was more than offset by the overwhelming advantage of water transport for carrying goods in bulk. As a 'free river', however, the Severn was exceptional, for throughout the Middle Ages the value of rivers for power generation and as a source of food was increasingly exploited at the expense of navigation. River channels became blocked by the impassable barriers of weirs constructed to hold back the water and divert it to turn mill wheels. Their unpolluted waters teemed with fish, particularly salmon, and the better to exploit this valuable source of food many fish weirs were built, often at the instigation of neighbouring monasteries. These were constructed in the form of a deep V across the river so as to funnel the fish towards the trap which was set in the apex. The trap itself might consist of a net or a series of 'putcheons', conical constructions of woven withies tapering to a closed end, a number of which were set in the frame of the weir. Such weirs were usually arranged with their apex downstream, but occasionally in tidal waters they were set the other way round so that fish were caught when the tide was making. Putcheon weirs may still be seen on the banks of the Severn below Gloucester, though naturally these do not stretch from bank to bank.[3] Ancient fishing weirs have survived most strongly on Irish rivers.[4]

The fact that rivers were natural barriers to overland communications also helped to create new hazards, if not positive obstructions, for the inland navigator. Fords frequently took the form of man-made underwater causeways over which there was insufficient draught for navigation except at times of high water and the medieval bridges built to replace the fords created hazards of a different kind. Their many piers so obstructed the bed of the river that a very rapid current was generated under their arches. Old London Bridge was notorious in this respect, so much so that eminent personages when travelling on London river were customarily put ashore, leaving to their watermen the perils of shooting London Bridge. Again, so narrow and low-pitched were the arches of these bridges that even a moderate flood made headroom insufficient for navigation.

The expansion of trade—which the many mills themselves helped to create—brought increasing pressure for the improvement of river navigation which encountered stiff opposition from these other vested interests and it became extremely difficult to reconcile the different uses of rivers, all of them equally valuable to the medieval community.

Improvements to river navigation were at first of an elementary kind which did not conflict with milling or fishing interests because they did not attempt to extend its range. They consisted of cutting back the inside of acute bends, dredging out shoals and shallows, piling where the banks were weak, and weed cutting. On the Upper Thames dredging was known as ballasting[5] and the method by which this operation was carried out on the Thames in the nineteenth century may well have been a survival of ancient technique. As the illustration (Plate 4) shows, a long-handled scoop and a winch were outrigged from the gunwale of a simple wooden punt with a crew of two. While one man held down the blade of the scoop with a vertical pole to make it bite, the other wound in on the winch until the contents of the scoop or 'spoon' could be conveniently tipped into the boat. Later manually operated 'spoon dredgers' used on canals, in which the 'spoon' was slung from the jib of a small crane mounted on the dredger, were an obvious improvement upon this primitive arrangement.

For bank protection, piles, usually of alder poles 'in the round' were driven home by hand with mawls. A similar horizontal waling of poles was secured on the river side of the piles a foot from the top and tied to the bank of hand-made wrought iron ties. The area behind the piling was then filled in and topped up with marl.[6]

Weed cutting was carried out by a method which has survived to this day, being frequently used on canals. A number of scythe blades, linked together by chain, were hauled along the bed of the river by men on its banks. A temporary wooden boom was laid across the river downstream of the operation to trap the weed as it floated down so that it could be conveniently raked out.

All these operations not only helped navigation but checked flooding and the damage so caused, thus benefiting all river users. It was only when those concerned to improve navigation began to introduce fixed or movable devices designed to deepen available draught by holding back the water or to enable craft to pass fixed weirs, that they came into conflict with mill owners fearful of losing the supply to their mill wheels. The mill owners were joined in their opposition, not only by the owners of fishing weirs, but by neighbouring landowners who feared that by holding back the water the 'navigators' would increase the risk of flooding.

The earliest means by which the difference in level caused by a fixed weir was overcome was by making a portion of the weir removable to leave a passage sufficiently wide for boats to pass. Weirs so adapted were called variously flash locks, navigation weirs, water gates and, in East Anglia particularly, staunches. To the confusion of historians, many early writers refer to them simply as 'locks', a term now used exclusively to mean a pound lock with its two sets of gates. Early navigation weirs took different forms depending on the region and the date of their erection. The oldest and commonest type consisted of two substantial horizontal wooden members spanning the opening in the weir. The lower of these was of elm and was fixed firmly in the bed of the river, usually bedded in masonry, while the upper one was movable and positioned above high flood level. Against the upstream side of these main timbers there rested vertically a series of squared timbers of smaller section called 'rimers'. Against these rimers there rested in turn a series of boards attached to long wooden handles so that they could readily be withdrawn. These were known as 'paddles'. In a shallow weir, only one set of these paddles might be necessary, but if the fall was great a series of paddles might be superimposed. To open the weir, the procedure was first to remove the paddles successively, then the rimers, and finally the upper beam against which they bore. One of the earliest improvements was to pivot this beam at the bank and extend it landwards beyond its axis so that it was counterweighted. There was naturally a firmly based positive stop on the weir opposite the pivot to resist the action of the current. Such a swinging upper beam usually incorporated a timber footway for access to the paddles and rimers.

When the paddles and rimers had been withdrawn there was, as may be imagined, a considerable and violent fall of water which made the passage of a boat either up or down stream a pretty hazardous affair. A land-based winch was provided for the purpose of drawing up stream traffic through the weir, but in such cases it was usual to wait until the current had moderated somewhat. Downstream traffic, however, would 'shoot' the weir as soon as it was practicable, for it was a secondary function of the weir to provide a flush or 'flash' of water which would carry the boat over shallows in the reach downstream. Navigating a river equipped with many of these flash locks was as tedious as it was hazardous. It was made all the more so by the mill owners who, in most cases, only consented to the provision of flash locks at their weirs on condition that they controlled their opening. They were extremely reluctant to open them because the volume of water they released interfered with the working of their mills. Consequently, in order to obtain the maximum advantage from the opening of the flash locks, boats generally travelled in convoy. Even so, they were frequently stranded for weeks in dry summer seasons, for in such conditions the millers would refuse to draw their weirs.

On the Upper Thames between Oxford and Lechlade six navigation weirs of paddle and rimer type, known as Limbre's, Shifford, Duxford, Tenfoot, Thames, and Tadpole, existed until 1898 when the present Shifford Lock and cut were opened. Radcot Lock, built in 1892, had previously replaced two more weirs called Old Nan's and Old Man's. Medley, King's, Eynsham, and Eaton weirs were the last to survive on the Upper Thames. The average fall of these weirs was from a foot to eighteen inches, but King's weir, above Godstow fell 2 ft 6 in and was described in 1883 as 'difficult to manage'.

The way in which the Thames Conservancy regulated these weirs gives us an insight into the way traffic was handled on navigable rivers in the seventeenth century. H. R. Robertson,[7] writing in 1875, describes it as follows:

When the water is low, the river is flashed twice a week by the regularly appointed keepers of the weirs, each of them waiting till the water from the weir next up the stream has reached him. By this means a continually augmenting volume of water descends, on the flood of which the whole of the traffic is carried. Sometimes the bargemen are sorely tempted to draw a flash on their own account, when they may have been unusually delayed, or are for any reason particularly anxious to proceed. However, the Thames Conservators are severe, and have issued hand-bills stating that all persons offending in the above case render themselves liable to a penalty of £20, and the strict observance of the regulations is considered so essential that the prosecution of offenders is deemed by them an imperative duty.

An obvious development of the old paddle and rimer type of weir was the water gate in which the rimers were no longer detachable but were fixed to the upper swinging beam of the weir and to a lower horizontal member that butted against the lower fixed beam or 'sill' of the weir. In this way the rimers became the vertical framing of a large swinging gate and the winch which had been provided to assist boats upstream was now used to open the gate against the current. The wooden paddles in this gate type of weir were no longer removable but could only be slid up and down in the gate frame. The wooden uprights attached to them carried a row of holes so that the paddles could be levered up by means of a handspike.

Water gates of this type survived at Pensham, near Pershore, and Cropthorne on the Warwickshire Avon until recently when they and their accompanying masonry weirs were swept away in course of the improvements made to the navigation by the Lower Avon Navigation Trust.

Although the water gate may seem at first thought an improvement on the primitive arrangement, in practice it had disadvantages. It may have been safer, but it was certainly slower and it consumed more water to less effect. It was impossible to winch open the gate against any considerable head of water and consequently upstream traffic must needs wait with water running to waste until the waters above and below the weir had almost made a level. For the same reason, boats bound downstream lost the benefit of a 'flash' to speed them on their way. It is therefore a misnomer to call a water gate a flash lock since it was incapable of assisting passage over downstream shallows to any appreciable extent. So far as this writer is aware, the water gate type of weir was not used on sites where there were existing mills. The water consumed in working them was unlikely to endear them to mill owners and it is significant that both the Avon water gates were built on sites remote from mills for the express purpose of raising the water level over shallows immediately above them.

The typical East Anglian staunch was a better solution to the problem and it therefore possessed a greater survival value. According to de Salis, writing in 1904,[8] of the thirty-three navigation weirs then surviving in England, twenty-seven were staunches in East Anglia. There were then, according to this authority, three on the Great Ouse between Bedford and Offord, eight and five respectively on its tributaries the Little Ouse and Larke, one on Lakenheath Lode and ten on the Nene between Peterborough and Northampton. These staunches sometimes held up considerable reaches of water. For example, Crosswater Staunch, the lowest on the Little Ouse, held up four miles and Orton Staunch, on the Nene two miles above Peterborough, three miles. In such cases, when the water was low, boats might be held at the staunch for as long as a week waiting for the water in the long reach above to make up sufficiently. To avoid such delays lighters trading on the Nene carried 'staunching tackle' with them. This consisted of stout stakes, wattled hurdles and a large canvas sheet. An empty lighter would be moored broadside across the river and with the aid of this tackle a temporary dam or staunch would be built.

A typical East Anglian staunch amounted, in effect, to a single huge paddle in a stout timber frame which could be lifted vertically like a guillotine to a sufficient height to enable boats to pass beneath. They were raised by means of a wooden-barrelled winch and chain mounted in the framing overhead. Although some of these staunches were built as late as the nineteenth century, their design is of very ancient origin. They derive almost certainly from the many sluices of guillotine type built by Cornelius Vermuyden and his Dutch engineers, on the model most commonly used in their own country, when they carried out their great drainage works in the Fens. These they completed in 1652. Vermuyden's sluices were for water control only, but his design was adapted when it became necessary to improve the Fenland rivers for navigation. Vermuyden himself created this necessity, for, by building his great sluice at Denver,* he stemmed the tides at this point, and craft which had hitherto made use of them to navigate the old channel of the Great Ouse, the Little Ouse and the Lark could no longer do so.

*Denver Sluice was blown up by a violent tide in 1713 and was rebuilt in 1748 by the Swiss architect Labelye.

Crosswater Staunch on the Little Ouse at Botany Bay, near the junction of Lakenheath Lode, probably originated in the immediate post Denver Sluice period and may have been intended to allow navigation in the river to continue to Brandon, if not to Thetford. It proved inadequate and seven additional staunches were built on the river at a much later date. These have been fully described by R. H. Clark.[9] Whereas Crosswater Staunch was removed in 1917, those of later date survived until the 1930s, although no longer used for navigation. Three were rebuilt purely for water control purposes by the Catchment Board, who then became responsible for the river, and the remaining four were removed to leave an open channel. These staunches were built between 1827 and 1835, four of them by Charles Burrell & Sons of Thetford. In the case of six of them the winch barrel which drew up the sluice door was turned through reduction gearing by a large wooden wheel 13 ft 2 in in diameter with spokes projecting through the rim like a ship's steering wheel. There was no ratchet and pawl; to hold the staunch in the open position a hook on a length of chain was placed on one of the wheel spokes. At Crosswater and Croxton staunches the large wheel was omitted. They were opened by a detachable handle or 'windlass', an extra pair of reduction gears being added to supply the necessary leverage.

A delightful painting of a Little Ouse staunch by F. W. Watts, a contemporary of Constable, is reproduced on Plate 2. As will be seen from this, the sluices used to regulate the flow of water through the weir operate on the same guillotine principle as the staunch itself but on a smaller scale. Such sluices have been called 'clows' in the Fenlands ever since Vermuyden's day. The term is also used in Yorkshire where it is spelled 'clough' and applied to the paddles or sluices of canal locks. The staunch in Watts's picture is shown closed against the boat. When fully drawn it allowed a navigable headroom varying from 8 ft 6 in at Brandon to 11 ft at Thetford.

Apart from the Thames where navigation weirs were in use as early as 1585, the Great Ouse was the first river in England upon which considerable improvement works were carried out expressly for the purpose of navigation, including the construction of staunches. Arnold Spencer (1587–1655) of Cople in Bedfordshire was the man responsible. Professor Skempton classes Spencer as an 'Engineer-Undertaker'[10] since he appears to have been a man of substance who not only devised and superintended the improvements but also financed them.

Spencer set to work to improve the Great Ouse between St Ives and St Neots, a stretch of sixteen miles, in 1628, his authority to do so being a Patent granted to him by Charles I on 3 January 1627 which empowered him 'to make other rivers, streams and waters navigable and passable for boats, keeles and other vessels to pass from place to place', he to have the sole right to use his own methods or 'engines' on payment of £5 per annum to the Exchequer and to retain the profits on rivers so improved for a term of eighty years. This Patent was originally granted for eleven years but was subsequently extended to twenty-one years.[11]

Spencer appears to have completed his work on the St Ives–St Neots section, including six 'sluices', in from three to four years, but his ambition was to make the river navigable to Bedford. To this end he built another staunch above Eaton Mills and dredged the river to Great Barford, but he never achieved his ambition, although there was quite a considerable trade on the river up to Great Barford during the seven years preceding the outbreak of the Civil War. Spencer may also have carried out some work on the Essex Stour since he received rights in that river in 1638.[12]

In 1674 Henry Ashley senior (c. 1630–1700) leased the Great Ouse Navigation, and from this date until the end of the century he and his son, Henry Ashley junior (c. 1654–1730), not only restored Spencer's works, which had fallen into decay during the war, but carried out considerable improvements of their own. This despite a protracted and bitter legal feud with the Jemmatt family to whom Spencer had assigned his patent rights. Owing to Vermuyden's Fen drainage scheme there was no longer sufficient depth of water at St Ives so a new staunch was built just below that place. The navigation up to Great Barford was improved by building two new sluices, three staunches and a short artificial cut. By 1689 the Ashleys had fulfilled Spencer's ambition by making the river navigable for a further seven miles to Bedford. In this section there were three new sluices. This venture proved profitable to the Ashleys, bringing them an income from tolls of £400 p.a., a not inconsiderable sum at that time.

The younger Ashley also improved the navigation of the River Lark between Mildenhall and Bury St Edmunds, but in this case he acted as engineer only, the navigation rights being assigned to the local gentry.

It will have been noted that in the account of this work on the Ouse, the terms 'sluice' and 'staunch' are differentiated. Here we run into the difficulty of terminology. By this date 'sluice' might well mean a pound lock, but this is as far as we can go where the Great Ouse is concerned. We cannot be certain.

Pound locks were a product of the Italian Renaissance, but it was not until the end of the sixteenth century or the beginning of the seventeenth that the idea crossed the Alps. It may be, however, that there was parallelism in invention, for the navigation weir of water gate type represented one half of a pound lock and it was only necessary to build two such weirs close together to have a primitive form of pound lock, the short reach of the river between them forming the pound. There is evidence in England to suggest that the modern pound lock may indeed have originated in this way by evolution rather than invention. It is said that the pounds of the ancient locks on the Bedfordshire Ivel between Shefford and Tempsford were enclosed, not by gates, but by rimers and paddles, flash lock fashion, but whether any remains survive to confirm this is not known. Again, a very curious lock existed on the Thames at Sutton Courtenay until 1809 when this reach of the river was by-passed by the present Clifton Cut and Culham Lock. In the seventeenth century this consisted of two flash locks, one at the head and one at the tail of Sutton Pool, which thus became, in effect, the lock pound. There is a sixteenth-century reference to two flash locks at Sutton Courtenay so this arrangement may have been of very ancient origin. As Sutton Pool was used to work a mill the reason for this arrangement is obscure, since it must have interfered seriously with the working of the mill and it is not surprising that the mill's owners levied an exceptionally heavy toll on barge traffic. They were paid £3,000 compensation by the Thames Commissioners when Culham Lock was built.[13]

The curious shape of the chambers of some old river locks, although they are now of masonry, may point to the fact that they originally formed part of the natural bed of the river. Cherry Ground Lock, on the River Lark, six miles below Bury St Edmunds was in the shape of a crescent moon, and on the Warwick Avon Wyre and Cleeve locks are diamond shaped while Luddington Upper Lock is circular. On the Rivers Wey and Kennet Navigations there are to be seen locks in which the pound consists of sloping grass banks, only that part in the immediate vicinity of the gates being timber piled. Such survivals are rare. There was a serious loss of water by percolation through the banks, added to which special provision had to be made to prevent boats settling onto the banks as the lock emptied. Consequently, locks with vertically walled masonry chambers of modern form began to appear in England in the seventeenth century.

The earliest recorded pound locks in England were on the Exeter Canal, a short lateral cut beside the River Exe which was built between 1564 and 1567 by 'John Trew of Glamorgan, gentleman' who received a fee of £200 and was granted tolls. Although this was an isolated improvement of limited scale, its conception was advanced in that it foreshadowed the many artificial cuts by which river navigations were improved in the eighteenth century. A weir was built across the Exe to divert water into the cut at its upstream end and there were three pound locks with 'basins' (chambers) 189 ft long by 23 ft wide capable of passing several boats at one lockage. The reason for this generous provision was that the tail of the cut was only navigable for a short period around high tide. The upper ends of the locks were closed by twin mitre gates of modern form, each fitted with three sluices or 'paddles', but the lower gates, curiously enough, were single and must have been massive affairs.

The next pound lock to be built in England at Waltham Abbey on the River Lea in 1571–74 had two sets of mitre gates and this became standard practice in England except on narrow canal locks where the single upper gate became standard and single lower gates were occasionally used.

More significant were the three pound locks at Iffley, Sandford, and Swift Ditch, which were built in 1632 to improve navigation on the difficult reach of the Thames between Oxford and Burcot which had a fall of 30 ft in fifteen miles. At the time they were building Twyne visited Exeter and made a plan of John Trew's locks which he showed to the Thames Commissioners. This drawing, now with the Twyne-Langbaine MSS in the Bodleian Library, is the earliest extant plan of an English lock. However, says Twyne, 'the carpenters had newely begun their sluices another waye and so it was not heeded'.[14] The Thames locks had mitre gates at each end, so perhaps the lock at Waltham Abbey was their model.

These early Thames locks had masonry chambers measuring, according to Thacker, 80 ft long by 20 ft wide and were of far better construction than those built lower down the river under an improvement Act of 1770 which were mainly of timber and required rebuilding after a few years. The locks at Iffley and Sandford have long since been replaced by modern locks, but the remains of the ancient chamber of the third, dammed at one end, can still be seen near the head of the Swift Ditch. This Ditch was once the main channel of the river until the monks of Abingdon diverted it for the 'convenience and cleanliness' of their Abbey. But the Oxford–Burcot improvers decided to make the Swift Ditch their navigable channel, and so it remained until the present Abingdon Lock and Cut was opened in 1790 and the old lock fell into disuse.

Despite the existence of these three pound locks of modern type at so early a date, the Thames continued for many years to be beset by numerous flash locks, some of them believed to date back to 1200. Apart from the longest lived examples on the river above Oxford, there were fifteen flash locks between London and Oxford, the majority of which were not superseded until the 1790s. The fact that on the Thames, as on other English rivers, the flash lock survived the coming of the pound lock by so many years was not due solely to the cost of replacement but to illogical prejudice against pound locks on the part of the mill owners who argued that they would consume more of their precious water than flash locks. The practice of opening a series of flash locks in sequence at stated times and thereby passing a large convoy of barges through together may have caused delays to river traffic but it suited the mill owners who controlled the flash locks. They argued that the substitution of pound locks would mean that barges would lock through individually, using more water than before. This argument was of doubtful validity, but one truth undoubtedly influenced them. Like a weir of water gate type, the normal working of a pound lock does not provide a 'flash'. Short of steps to deepen river channels, the mill owners doubtless feared that the use of pound locks would mean that bargemen would leave the paddles up, not only at the locks but on the adjacent weirs, to secure the necessary flash. The only compromise was to make the chamber of the pound lock sufficiently large to accommodate a convoy of barges and then to regulate the traffic as formerly. This cannot have proved a satisfactory solution to the never ending battle over water supplies, but it may explain the curious lock at Sutton Courtenay.

In fact, by holding back the water permanently, the pound lock presented by far the better proposition where the mill owner was concerned provided the bargemen did not have to resort to flashing. William Sandys (c. 1600–c. 1670) evidently realized this and was able to convince the mill owners to that effect when he engineered the navigation of the Warwick Avon from Tewkesbury to Bidford in 1636–39. At each mill weir he constructed a pound lock and provided navigation weirs of water gate type to assist craft over shallows in the reaches between, such as the old ford at Cropthorne near the site of Jubilee Bridge. The purpose of these water gates, sited where they were, was twofold; first, they obviated the need for 'flashing' from the mill weirs and locks; secondly, when not being used for the passage of craft, their gates stood open so that the miller at the tail of the reach could not complain that the length of headwater he drew upon had been permanently reduced.

A member of a wealthy landowning Worcestershire family, William 'Water-work' Sandys, as he came to be called, was, like Arnold Spencer, an engineer-undertaker, not only planning the work on Avon but financing it. His subsequent work on the Teme was interrupted by the Civil War, but after the war was over he undertook to make the Wye and Lug navigable in concert with other members of his family. Of the same class was John Mallet, a country gentleman of Somerset who undertook the navigation of the rivers Parret and Tone in 1638, and Sir Richard Weston (1591–1652) of Sutton, Surrey, who engineered the Wey Navigation from the Thames at Weybridge to Guildford between 1651 and 1653.

The Wey Navigation is generally considered the finest work of its kind to be built in the seventeenth century. To overcome a fall of 86 ft between Guildford Wharf and the Thames, Weston built ten pound locks and four weirs, but what is more significant is that out of a total length of fifteen miles, seven miles consist of artificial cut. Previous undertakers had shown a reluctance to make extensive cuts, following the natural course of the river as much as possible. They hesitated to incur the additional labour and expense, not only of digging the cuts, but of constructing the necessary overbridges which such new works usually entailed. Weston built twelve new bridges in the course of his Wey improvements, and his work was the prototype for many of the more ambitious river navigation works which would be carried out during the first sixty years of the next century.

One other significant seventeenth century figure deserves to be mentioned and that is Andrew Yarranton (1616–84). Although he would not have so styled himself, Yarranton was a civil engineer who, although he evidently possessed some capital of his own, carried out

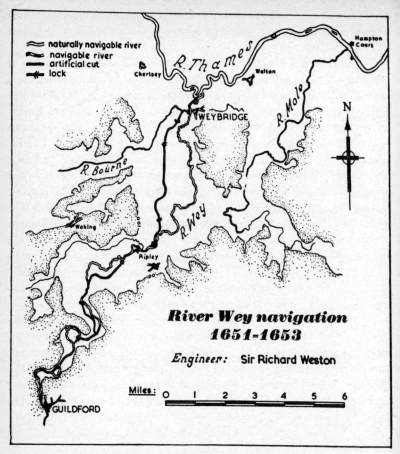

naturally navigable river
navigable river
artificial cut
lock

Chertsey

R.Thames

Walton

Hampton Court

WEYBRIDGE

R.Mole

R. Bourne

N

Woking

R.Wey

Ripley

100'

River Wey navigation 1651-1653

Engineer: Sir Richard Weston

Miles: 0 1 2 3 4 5 6

GUILDFORD

work on behalf of other capitalists or 'undertakers'. Thus he was
engaged to make the Worcestershire Stour navigable from Stourbridge
to Kidderminster in 1662, completing the work in 1665 with Lord
Windsor as the chief financial undertaker. This was only a small part of
Yarranton's ambitious scheme to unite the Severn with the Trent, but
no further progress was made. Despite Yarranton's advocacy of such
works in his book *England's Improvement by Sea and Land*, published
in 1677, the times were not yet ripe. Yarranton was also associated with
Lord Windsor in the work of extending Sandys's Avon Navigation
from Bidford to Stratford and in an abortive attempt to make the River
Salwarpe navigable from the Severn up to Droitwich. He also prepared

a plan for a new cut to restore the Dee Navigation to Chester, which would be carried out in modified form by Nathaniel Kinderley some sixty years later.

Working on his own account, Yarranton established an ironworks at his native Astley near the west bank of the Severn below Stourport and locked the Dick Brook to provide access to his works from the Severn. This was in 1652 and was therefore his first navigation work. Extensive remains of two of his lock chambers survive on the brook to provide an enigma for industrial archaeologists. J. M. Palmer and M. I. Berrill, who explored the site in 1958,[15] concluded that these locks had only possessed gates at the lower end and were therefore not pound locks but navigation weirs. This does not explain the reason for the massive masonry chambers which, by their own reckoning, measure 10 ft 9 in wide and 70 ft long, a feature not found on any navigation weir because it was unnecessary. Another puzzling feature is that the Dick Brook on which these locks are situated is so narrow and tortuous as to make navigation by any sizeable craft impossible. This writer has suggested[16] as a possible solution to this mystery the use by Yarranton of small 'tub boats' such as were subsequently used extensively in Shropshire.

In the case of many works of seventeenth-century waterway engineering it is impossible to say with certainty that they have not been modified in some way by repairs or in the course of subsequent navigation or drainage works. But in the great sandstone blocks of the Dick Brook lock chambers we have undoubtedly a memorial of Andrew Yarranton, one of the first waterway engineers. He has bequeathed to posterity an intriguing problem.

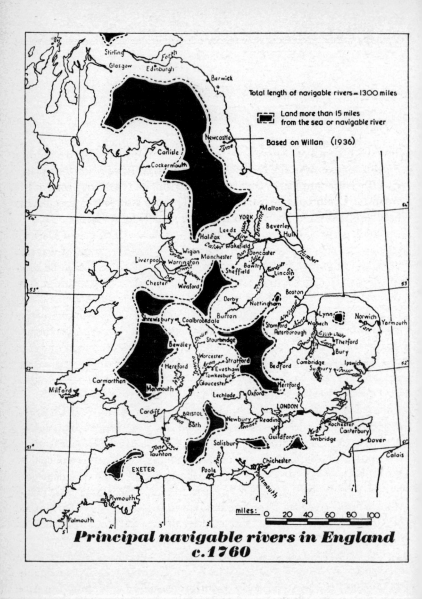

Principal navigable rivers in England c.1760

Total length of navigable rivers = 1300 miles

Land more than 15 miles from the sea or navigable river

Based on Willan (1936)

miles: 0 20 40 60 80 100

CHAPTER TWO

Towards the Canal Era,
1700-1760

The eighteenth century was not far advanced before two highly significant events in the history of the Industrial Revolution took place. In 1709 Abraham Darby first successfully smelted iron with coke at his works at Coalbrookdale, and in 1712 Thomas Newcomen erected his first recorded atmospheric steam engine near Dudley Castle.

These seeds of change were slow to germinate. The use of Darby's process was for long confined to the making of cast iron and it was not until the invention of the reverbatory furnace that coal could be used in the making of wrought iron. Similarly, Newcomen's steam engine was designed solely as a mine pump. It could not be adapted successfully to provide rotative motion so that for driving machinery the waterwheel remained the only practicable source of power. Nevertheless, by enabling coal to be got from deeper levels, Newcomen's engine supplied ironmasters and other manufacturers with an increasing amount of fuel to supplement supplies of charcoal which were dwindling owing to the wholesale denudation of woodlands.

As a result, there was a slow but steady expansion of trade throughout the first half of the eighteenth century which spelled increasing pressure for the improvement of internal transport. Because water transport was uniquely cheap and convenient for the carriage of coal in bulk, more and more rivers were made navigable for boats of useful burden, often at considerable capital cost in making locks and cuts. These works were carried out by professional engineers like Andrew Yarranton. With one significant exception, wealthy undertaker-engineers such as Sir Richard Weston had no successors in the eighteenth century.

The Aire & Calder Navigation was the first considerable work to be completed in the new century. The River Aire was naturally navigable to Weeland at this time and the work consisted of extending the Aire navigation to Leeds and making its tributary the Calder navigable from its junction with the Aire near Castleford to Wakefield. Between

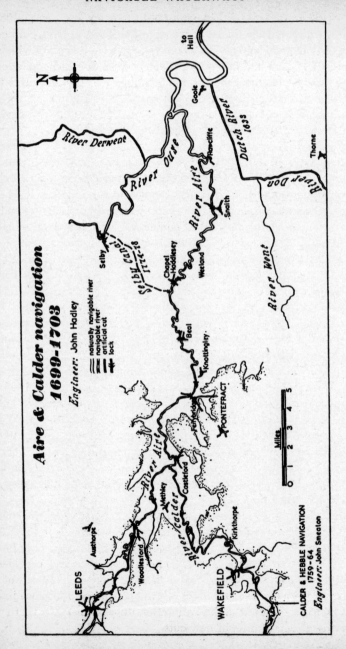

Aire & Calder navigation
1699-1703

Engineer: John Hadley

naturally navigable river
navigable river
artificial cut
lock

River Derwent

River Ouse

River Aire

Selby Canal 1774-78

to Hull

Goole

Rawcliffe

Snaith

Dutch River 1635

Thorne

River Don

River Went

Selby

Chapel Haddlesey

Wetland

Beal

Knottingley

Ferrybridge

PONTEFRACT

Castleford

Methley

Woodlesford

Austhorpe

River Aire

River Calder

Kirkthorpe

LEEDS

WAKEFIELD

CALDER & HEBBLE NAVIGATION
1759-64

Engineer: John Smeaton

Miles
0 1 2 3 4 5

Weeland and Leeds ten locks were built to overcome a rise of 68 ft in thirty miles. On the Calder there were four locks in twelve miles, the rise to Wakefield being 28 ft. There were five lateral cuts of which two, one on the Aire and one on the Calder, were of considerable length. The masonry lock chambers were 56 ft long by 19 ft wide with 3 ft 6 in of water over the sills, being built to suit the Humber or Yorkshire Keels, the type of craft previously used on the naturally navigable portions of the rivers radiating from the Humber.

The engineer of the Aire & Calder was John Hadley of whom little is known except that he is referred to by a contemporary as 'that great Master of Hydraulicks',[1] and that he patented a device for raising and lowering an undershot waterwheel in accordance with the level of the stream. He was responsible for several water supply schemes and may have been a Midlander, for in connection with one such scheme at Worcester he is referred to as 'John Hadley of West Bromwich'.

Hadley surveyed the rivers in December 1697 accompanied by the then Mayor of Leeds and Ralph Thoresby, who wrote in his diary for 4 December 1697: 'Down the river to Weland, observed the sands etc., and upon the whole, the ingenious Mr Hadley questions not its being done, and with less charge than expected, affirming it the noblest river he ever saw not already navigable.'[2] Hadley later attended the House of Commons Committee on the Navigation Bill which received the Royal Assent in May 1699. He was then appointed engineer in charge at the munificent salary of 400 guineas and completed the work in 1703.

Inland navigation in this area was subsequently improved by another little-known engineer, this time a native of York named William Palmer who extended the River Don navigation from Barnby to three miles below Sheffield at Tinsley. Palmer also deepened the Yorkshire Ouse to York by contracting its bed so that the scouring action of the current was increased. Both these works were carried out between 1726 and 1732.

By far the most ambitious work to be carried out in the south of England in the first half of the eighteenth century was the Kennet Navigation from the Thames at Reading to Newbury, if only because the fall of the River Kennet, 85 in to the mile, was considerably greater than any of the rivers so far mentioned. This meant that eighteen pound locks had to be built to overcome a difference in level of 138 ft in eighteen-and-a-half miles. In this distance there were eleven-and-a-half miles of new cuts.

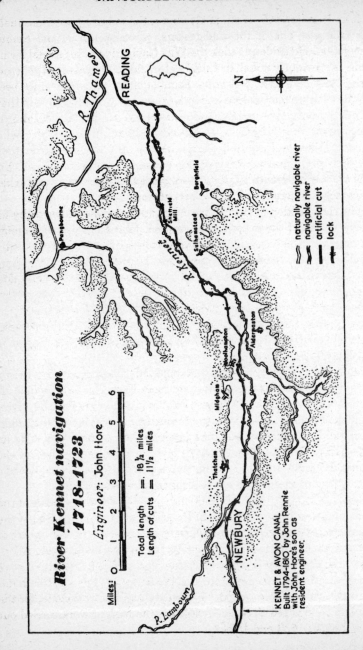

River Kennet navigation
1718-1723

Engineer: John Hore

Miles: 0 1 2 3 4 5 6

Total length = 18½ miles
Length of cuts = 11½ miles

KENNET & AVON CANAL
Built 1794-1810 by John Rennie
with John Hore's son as
resident engineer.

naturally navigable river
navigable river
artificial cut
lock

N

READING

R. Thames

Pangbourne

Burghfield

Sheffield
Mill

Southcote

R. Kennet

Aldermaston

Woolhampton

Midgham

Thatcham

NEWBURY

R. Lambourn

John Hore (c.1690–1762) of Newbury, the son of a prosperous maltster who was one of the undertakers, was engineer of the Kennet Navigation. He evidently took the Wey Navigation as his model for his locks, as previously noted, had sloping turf sides. They were of generous size: 122 ft long and 19 ft wide. Some of these locks have since been rebuilt with smaller masonry chambers, though others survive in their original state. The construction of the new cuts involved the building of many new overbridges, most of which were timber-built swing bridges. These were no doubt the cheapest solution, for apart from their low first cost, the need for approach embankments was obviated. But they were a hindrance to navigation, particularly in later years when the waterway became part of a through route.

The construction of the Kennet Navigation was also noteworthy for the bitterness of the opposition it aroused. John Hore had to contend, not only against the mill owners who, as usual, feared for their water supplies, but with organized opposition from the town of Reading, which had hitherto handled the waterborne trade of the area and now feared the loss of a substantial portion of that trade to Newbury. Hore had to contend against organized gangs under the leadership of the Mayor and Recorder of Reading, who molested his workers and broke down the newly finished locks. Nevertheless the work was begun in 1718 and finished by 1723.

John Hore subsequently became engineer in charge of the Bristol Avon Navigation, sixteen miles long, from Bristol to Bath, which he carried out between 1725 and 1727. He also surveyed the rivers Stroudwater and Chelmer, in the former case proposing a canal eight miles long for which an Act was obtained, but nothing was done on either river. His son, born in 1730, became resident engineer of the Kennet & Avon Canal under John Rennie, so the Hore family played a notable part in the construction of this coast to coast route.

Before leaving the south of England, mention should be made of the River Medway. 'The Company of Proprietors of the Navigation of the River Medway' owed their existence to an Act of 1664, but an Act of 1740 empowered this body to improve the navigation between Maidstone and Tonbridge, mainly with the object of reducing the cost of carriage of timber supplies from the Weald to the Navy at Chatham. The engineer is not known, nor is the extent of the work done, for the Medway Navigation as we see it today is the fruit of work carried out under Acts of 1802 and 1824.[3]

North-west England, that area of south Lancashire and north Cheshire so soon destined to be the cradle of both canals and railways, became an important centre of river improvement activity. The rivers Mersey, Irwell, Weaver and Douglas all received attention between the years 1722 and 1742.

Thomas Steers (1672–1750) had surveyed the rivers Mersey and Irwell from Bank Quay at Warrington to Manchester, in 1712, an Act authorizing the work was passed in 1721 and it was completed about 1725. There were eight locks in a distance of fifteen miles to overcome a rise to Manchester of 52 ft. Steers was one of the company of undertakers and it is generally believed that he acted as engineer. Steers was also responsible for the Douglas Navigation which was completed from the Ribble Estuary to Wigan after four years' work in 1742. More significantly, he engineered the Newry Canal in Northern Ireland which presaged the coming canal age and will be mentioned in the context of the next chapter. Though little known today, Thomas Steers was, as Professor Skempton has said,[4] one of the notable civil engineers of England. He not only carried out considerable dock works at Rotherhithe and Liverpool but also practised as an architect like Telford, Mylne and other engineers of the canal era.

Between 1730 and 1732 the River Weaver was made navigable up to Winsford, a distance of twenty miles, and eleven locks were built to overcome a rise of 42 ft. Thomas Robinson, of whom nothing else is known, was appointed 'surveyor general of the works' and acted as resident engineer. He continued to hold his position on the Weaver until 1735 during which time various minor improvements were made. But the state of the Weaver Navigation was evidently not all it should have been for in 1758 a protracted programme of improvements was embarked upon under the superintendence of Robert Pownall (1715–80) who had earlier worked on the Navigation as a clerk at Winsford. Pownall worked in association with another engineer, Henry Berry (1720–1812). Between them they were responsible for building a new lock at Northwich and new locks and cuts at Saltersford and Pickerings. Pownall's connection with the Weaver was lifelong and by the time of his death he had built four more locks and cuts on the river.

Henry Berry was assistant to Thomas Steers on the Newry Canal and was subsequently engineer of the Sankey Canal from the Mersey to St Helens. The work of these two men, Steers and Berry, therefore forms a link of continuity between the age of river navigations and the age of canals.

One other notable river navigation work was undertaken on the eve of the canal age. This was the Calder & Hebble Navigation from Wakefield to Salterhebble, near Halifax, and it may be said to represent the summit of engineering achievement in the art of river improvement to date. It is notable in two respects. First, the difference in level to be overcome was uniquely great, the Calder falling at the rate of 90 in to the mile, which amounted to a difference of level of 178 ft in the twenty-four miles of the navigation. Secondly, it was the work of John Smeaton, (1724–92) a name justly famous in the history of civil engineering in Britain. To call Smeaton the first British civil engineer may seem unfair to his less well known predecessors. Yet he seems to have been the first man so to describe himself, and by his stature and quality as a man, no less than by his achievements, Smeaton ensured the recognition of civil engineering as an established profession.

Smeaton's work on the Calder followed hard upon the undertaking for which he is best remembered today—the building of the Eddystone Lighthouse. In fact he first surveyed the Calder during the latter end of 1757 when winter storms had suspended his work on the lighthouse. He built twenty-six locks on the river and five-and-threequarter miles of new cut. For the lock walls, Smeaton used one of his newly discovered hydraulic limes. Joseph Nickalls, later to become one of the founder members of the Society of Civil Engineers, was Smeaton's resident engineer on the Calder.

It was no fault of Smeaton's that, following a great storm over the Pennines on the night of 7 October 1758, the worst floods for fifty years swept down the Calder and the Proprietors afterwards reported ruefully that 'the navigation is ruined so far as to be no longer passable for any kind of vessels from Wakefield to Brooksmouth, or from Brooksmouth to Salterhebble Bridge'.[5] The Company was subsequently re-formed and reconstruction authorized by an Act of 1769. Once again John Smeaton was the engineer, but this time his protégé, William Jessop, was appointed resident engineer under him.

Jessop succeeded Smeaton on the latter's retirement to acquire an engineering reputation second only to his mentor. In later life Jessop advised the Thames Commissioners on the improvement of the Thames between Dorchester and Lechlade, and in his advice on the subject of locks and cuts he followed the principles which his master

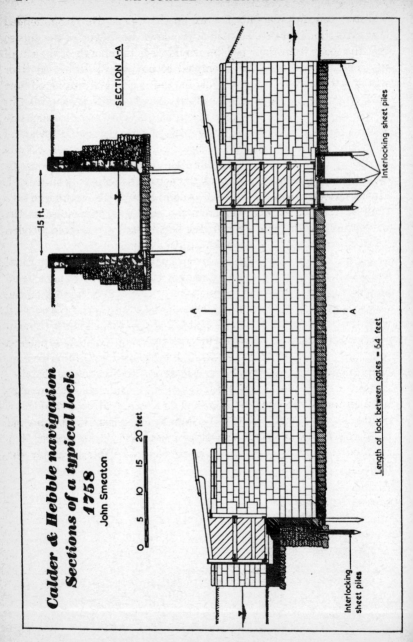

Calder & Hebble navigation
Sections of a typical lock
1758
John Smeaton

0 5 10 15 20 feet

SECTION A-A

15 ft.

Interlocking sheet piles

Interlocking sheet piles

Length of lock between gates = 54 feet

Smeaton had first put into practice on the Calder. He recommended that locks should always be sited at the downstream end of the cuts so that the scour from their paddles would clear the mouth of the cut of silt. Those who have ever attempted to navigate a little-used river will appreciate the wisdom of this, for they will have discovered how quickly a river will deposit a bar of silt across the downstream mouths of the lock cuts. Jessop further recommended that the masonry side walls of the lock chambers should be specially constructed to resist lateral pressure, always a problem in lock construction. That Smeaton was one of the first engineers to appreciate this problem is clear from his design for the Calder locks in which the side walls are heavily buttressed. Finally, Jessop advocated sluices or paddles of large size in order to save time in lockage. In this connection the large ground paddles on the Calder locks, with their toothed rack bars raised by a pivoted wooden lever, may well be of Smeaton's original design.

This, then, was the 'state of the art' at the beginning of the canal age, the culmination of a process of slow but sure improvement based on growing experience that began with Arnold Spencer's work on the Great Ouse in 1618. The two maps reproduced here, in which land more than fifteen miles from navigable water is marked black, show in graphic form the extent of the progress made by 1760. It is evident from the 1760 map, however, that there was still no communication between the east and west coasts. Moreover, a great deal of Britain's mineral wealth, which new techniques were enabling men to exploit upon an increasing scale, was situated on the central watershed, most notably on that dividing the Severn from the Trent basins. Commercial pressure for improved communications was therefore unsatisfied, but by 1760 the money and the engineers were available to supply the remedy.

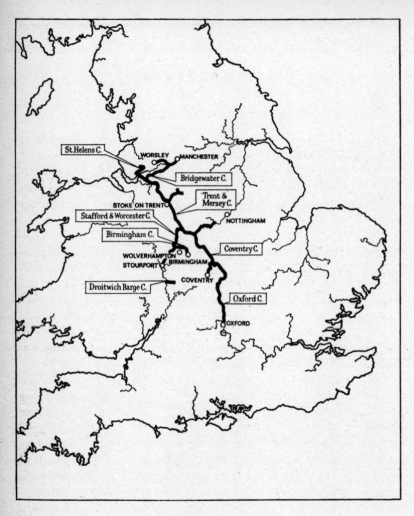

The first canals

CHAPTER THREE

The First Canals

Although the art of improving rivers for navigation by constructing pound locks and making artificial channels or cuts was well established, much more money and engineering expertise was required in order to construct wholly artificial waterways over high watersheds between river basins and so bring the advantage of cheap transport to the developing industrial areas of Britain.

One of the chief reasons for the outstanding success of the Coalbrookdale Ironworks, where the Darby family initiated so many significant pioneer developments, was that it was located on one of the very few sites in Britain where deposits of coal and iron ore lay adjacent to a navigable river—the Severn. We may be sure that the moral of this was not lost upon other ironmasters and manufacturers, particularly those whose undertakings were situated in the neighbouring highlands of Staffordshire. Here the exploitation of rich deposits of coal and ore was inhibited by the need to transport over land to the Severn or the Trent. In such a situation the construction of canals became inevitable, but the date of their inception was postponed until such time as a growing commerce could afford the large amount of capital required to finance such costly works. So far as technique was concerned, Britain lagged behind the continent of Europe. Many English noblemen, including the third Duke of Bridgewater, made a point of visiting the canals of Briare and Languedoc in the course of the Grand Tour. But although in this way these French canals may have been responsible for introducing the *idea* of canals to Britain they would appear to have had very little influence on British canal engineering technique. Physical conditions on a relatively small island and the availability of the necessary water supplies had a greater influence on native technique than continental models.

A glance at the central watershed of England reveals that it is in places so narrow that only the breadth of a field divides the sources of eastward and westward flowing rivers or their tributaries. This fortuitous conjunction led to several optimistic schemes for linking such rivers near their headwaters. As we have seen, Yarranton's Stour Navigation was intended to be a part of his scheme to unite Severn and Trent and the same engineer advocated a similar junction between Thames and Severn. The fact that the sources of the Waveney and the Little Ouse are only 25 ft apart led Francis Matthew in 1670, in a pamphlet entitled *A Mediterranean Passage by Water from London,*[1] to advocate their junction as part of a through water route from Great Yarmouth to York. But such ambitious proposals were ahead of their time and they overlooked two things, first the provision of sufficient water supply at these headwaters, and second that the course of a river in its uppermost reaches is by no means an ideal one from the point of view of navigation. It soon became obvious that topography prescribed an upper limit on rivers beyond which it was no longer a practicable proposition to render them navigable, and that the correct solution was to link such upper limits by an artificial channel and to tap as many of the headwater tributaries as possible to supply that channel with water.

The first canal in the British Isles to exemplify this principle, that is to say the first summit level canal, was the Newry Canal in Northern Ireland, constructed to facilitate the transport of coal from the Tyrone Collieries to Dublin. This had a summit level three miles long, mostly in rock cutting, which was supplied by a small reservoir fed by headwater streams. From the southern end of this summit the canal fell by locks 65 ft in nine miles to Newry, at the head of Carlingford estuary. At the opposite end of the summit the canal fell 22 ft in nine miles to Lough Neagh, there being a total of fifteen locks on the canal with chambers 60 ft by 15 ft and two larger sea locks at the terminals. Thomas Steers completed the survey in 1736 and superintended the work until 1741, when his place was taken by Acheson Johnson, who completed the canal in 1745.

It is significant that Henry Berry, the engineer of the Sankey Canal, worked as assistant to Steers on the Newry Canal. An Act of 20 March 1755 authorized the making of the Sankey Brook navigable from St Helens to its confluence with the Mersey near Widnes. Although he took part in the original survey on which this Act was based, Berry subsequently recommended that a canal should be built instead and supplied with water from the brook. His suggestion was adopted, and the work was subsequently carried out under his direction, although Priestley names John Eyes of Liverpool as the engineer.[2] An Act of April 1762 authorized an entrance lock from the Mersey at Fiddler's Ferry, but because this proved unsatisfactory on account of boats being neaped at the lock entrance the canal was subsequently extended for a little over three miles downstream to Widnes, where a new basin with twin entrance locks from the Mersey was constructed. As built, there were, according to Priestley, eight single locks with a fall of 6 ft each and two double locks with a fall of 15 ft each, the total fall from St Helens to the Mersey being 78 ft in a distance of ten miles, excluding the extension to Widnes. A total of eighteen swing bridges originally spanned the channel.

While it is strictly true to call the Sankey Canal the first in England, it was built in the river navigation tradition; that is to say it was, in effect, a long navigable cut, paralleling the course of the brook and drawing its water supply from it. Its construction confronted Berry with none of the engineering problems which were involved in building a high-level canal. Nevertheless it no doubt helped to inspire a far more significant project near by, the Bridgewater Canal which was built by a triumvirate consisting of Francis Egerton, third Duke of Bridgewater, his agent John Gilbert, and the engineer James Brindley.

The Bridgewater Canal originated from the need to provide a more economic transport outlet for the coal from the Worsley pits on the Bridgewater estate. This need had been apparent for many years, for in 1737 the third Duke's father had obtained an Act for making the Worsley brook navigable from Worsley Mill to its junction with the Irwell. Like the original Sankey brook scheme, however, this project lapsed and nothing was done until 1759, when the third Duke, obviously with the Sankey Canal project in mind, opted for a canal from Worsley Mill to join the Mersey at Hollin Ferry and obtained powers to construct it. Although a branch canal was subsequently built from Worsley onto Chat Moss in the direction of Hollin Ferry,[3] the Duke soon abandoned this plan due to his failure to reach agreement with the proprietors of the Mersey & Irwell Navigation. Instead, in association with Gilbert and Brindley, he conceived the far more ambitious scheme of carrying his canal into Manchester, a proposal which involved an aqueduct over the Irwell at Barton, with considerable approach embankments, including an embankment 900 yards long over Stretford Meadows. He obtained an Act authorizing construction exactly a year later, in March 1760. It was planned to supply the canal with water from a sough which drained the Duke's mines at Worsley, and although it would be level throughout and was not therefore a summit level canal, it involved civil engineering construction upon a scale hitherto unprecedented in England.

The Bridgewater Canal is notable in another respect. It remains the only considerable canal work to be carried out by one undertaker. Compared with river navigations, canals were so much more costly to construct that all major canal projects were thereafter undertaken by joint stock companies. To finance the building of his canal and its subsequent extension to the Mersey at Runcorn, the Duke raised money on the security of his great estates, the extent of his indebtedness rising, in January 1786, to the colossal peak of £346,805, representing a sum not far short of £3 million in our currency.

To call Francis Egerton, Duke of Bridgewater, the 'Father of Canals' is no mere figure of speech. He occupies a position unique in the transport history of these islands. Few individuals since his day have been in a position to raise and sustain such a financial burden; certainly no man since has possessed the courage to back so heavily a new and untried technical innovation. For so far as this country was concerned canals were wholly novel in 1760, too much so to attract the capital investment that was needed. We may say now as we survey the eighteenth-century scene in England that growing economic pressure made some radical improvement in inland transport inevitable, yet, but for the courage and conviction of one individual, the coming of canals might well have been postponed for a decade or more with far reaching effects on commercial growth.

It was many years before the Duke's gamble paid off, but when it did the reward was so great that it swung the mood of investors from 'wait and see' caution to the opposite of that over optimism which sparked off the speculative 'canal mania' of 1792. Because it was a private concern it is difficult to determine exactly how profitable the Bridgewater Canal was, though the net profit for 1803, the year of the Duke's death, has been given[4] as £65,952. Writing in 1831, Priestley states that income was estimated 'some years ago' at £130,000, and quotes a current figure of £260,000.[5] Yet the history of the Bridgewater Canal is a salutary one, for while its initial success ushered in the canal era, its inflated profits hastened the end of that era.

The reason why the Duke had to wait so long for his gamble to pay off was that he was opposed in principle to monopolies and monopolists. With a real sense of public obligation he bound himself to carry on his canals at low freight rates. For the same reason, when his old competitors, the proprietors of the Mersey & Irwell Navigation, finally threw up the sponge in 1776 and offered their concern to him for a mere £10,000, the Duke refused, saying bluntly that he had set out to break a monopoly, not to create one. Under the terms of the Duke's will, after his death the Bridgewater Canal was vested in a Trust managed by Captain Bradshaw, the late Duke's agent in succession to Gilbert. Bradshaw was a man typical of the new commercial spirit that was coming to the fore. He was what we should now describe euphemistically as a keen business man and his old master's philosophy simply did not make sense to one who thought only in terms of £.s.d. He bought out the 'old navigators' of the Mersey & Irwell for £550,800 and having thus created what he thought was a safe monopoly, raised canal freight rates threefold. Such shortsighted greed brought its inevitable nemesis. For it was their exasperation with Bradshaw's exactions that determined the merchants of Liverpool and Manchester to break his monopoly by building a railway between their two cities, with results that were far-reaching and fatal to canal interests everywhere. Faced with this threat, Bradshaw cut his freight rates by 55 per cent and ringed the Bridgewater Estate with armed men in a vain attempt to keep out George Stephenson and his surveyors. Too late; he had effectually killed the goose that had laid such golden eggs. Perhaps Bradshaw recalled ruefully a remark which his farsighted master had made in his old age: 'We shall do well enough if we can steer clear of those demmed tramroads.'

Just as the story of the Bridgewater Canal epitomizes the political and financial history of the canal era, so in its engineering it set an example for others to follow, for although it crossed no summit level, it was the first canal to take a course independent of rivers. Anyone who travels the length of the Bridgewater Canal today with a perceptive eye must agree that although subsequent canals may be longer and may boast more impressive individual works of engineering, they do not surpass this first canal in breadth of conception. First, it is lock-free for thirty miles from Worsley to Runcorn; secondly, the width of its channel reveals that it was laid out with wide boats in mind; thirdly, photographs of the original aqueduct over the Irwell at Barton taken shortly before it was demolished to make way for the Manchester Ship

Canal, reveal that early prints do not exaggerate and that it was indeed upon a larger scale than later, similar structures on the 'cross' of canals engineered by James Brindley. In this a remarkable parallel may be drawn between the Bridgewater Canal and the engineering of the first main railway lines, notably the London & Birmingham, which similarly surpassed the railways built subsequently.

The major share of the credit for the engineering of the Bridge-water canal is generally awarded to James Brindley, so that we may wonder why his later works, impressive though they are, in breadth of conception fail to equal the standard set by the Bridgewater. This is an excellent example of the way the history of past events may be radically altered by those who are not prepared to accept the judgment of earlier writers without checking them against original documents. For a recent study[6] of the Bridgewater Estate papers and of the records of the Bridgewater Canal has revealed that the Duke's agent, John Gilbert, played a far more predominant role in the conception, planning and actual construction of the canal than has been generally allowed. Nor was the role of the Duke merely that of a passive provider of capital. The partnership of the Duke, Gilbert and Brindley was so close and harmonious that it is impossible to determine which in-dividual partner should be awarded the greatest share of the credit. But if we look at the typical organization responsible for building subsequent canals and then apply the same organizational standards to the Bridgewater partnership, then it is Gilbert who emerges as survey-or and engineer-in-chief with James Brindley, the ingenious, illiter-ate craftsman, as resident engineer under him. Both were inspired by the Duke to give practical effect to his ideas.

It appears that it was Gilbert who was primarily responsible for the Barton aqueduct, the greatest single work of engineering on the origi-nal canal, while it was certainly Gilbert who proposed that the sough or adit which drained the Duke's mines at Worsley Delph should not only supply the canal with water but should be enlarged so that boats could proceed directly to the coal face to load, thus avoiding the necessity of hoisting the coal to the surface. By 1795 this underground canal system totalled fifteen miles, and it later attained a maximum extent of forty miles on two levels connected by an inclined plane of the type introduced by William Reynolds on the Ketley Canal in Shrop-shire. Although long disused for navigation, at least a part of this underground system still serves a drainage function and for this reason it is inspected at regular intervals by officials of the National Coal Board. The inclined plane survives relatively intact although it has not been used for many years.

Among men of spirit and enterprise the Duke's bold experiment attracted enormous interest, so that there were few who failed to visit the works at one time or another during construction. As soon as it became obvious to them that the new canal was going to be practically successful, it became equally obvious that this could be the answer to their own transport problems. The Duke's project had not proceeded far before an ambitious plan was born to link by canal the four great navigable rivers of England: Mersey, Trent, Severn and Thames, and joint stock companies were formed for the purpose of carrying it out. The key feature of this scheme was the Trent & Mersey Canal or 'Grand Trunk', with which canals to the Severn and the Thames would ultimately be linked. Foremost among the promoters of the Trent & Mersey was Josiah Wedgwood, the great potter of Burslem in north Staffordshire. Wedgwood had watched the progress of the Duke's experiment with the liveliest interest from the start since he recognized at once the immense value of a canal to his business, both for importing coal and raw materials and exporting the fragile finished product.

The entrepreneurs of this national canal project needed engineering 'know-how' and they looked to the Bridgewater Canal to supply it. As the Duke's agent, John Gilbert was wedded to his master's interests and was far too loyal a servant to be inveigled into other employment, not that there is any evidence that such an attempt was made. This left only one possible member of the Bridgewater triumvirate—James Brindley, and so it was that his is the name we primarily associate with that great 'cross' of canals that formed the skeleton around which England's midland waterway network developed.

From what little we know of the character of James Brindley he was far too honest and straightforward a man to make exaggerated claims for himself. But from now until his death no new canal scheme was considered viable until Mr Brindley had been consulted, and the eminence thus thrust upon an illiterate and unknown millwright no doubt accounts for the legend that he was wholly responsible for the engineering of the Bridgewater Canal. In 1831 Joseph Priestley wrote of: 'The Duke of Bridgewater, who, unassisted except by the natural genius of Brindley, carried into execution a series of difficult and expensive works which are, even at this time, unexampled.'[7] This attribution was later to be elaborated with a wealth of circumstantial detail by Samuel Smiles in his *Life* of James Brindley and so given a popular currency which has persisted to this day.

Priestley implies that not only the original Bridgewater Canal from Worsley to Manchester was the work of James Brindley, but also the long extension to the Mersey including what he describes as 'the stupendous embankment' across the valley of the River Bollin. Brindley was certainly engaged on the aqueduct carrying this extension over the Mersey to Stretford in 1763, but by 1767 when the Bollin embankment was building he was far too busily occupied with canal projects in the Midlands to pay more than very occasional visits to the North West. The embankment was raised by an engineer named Thomas Morris working under Gilbert's superintendence. Malet[8] quotes a letter written from Altrincham on 28 September 1767, which describes the building of this embankment and rebukes the recipient for awarding Brindley too much credit.

> The Duke of Bridgewater has another ingenious Man, Thomas Morris, who has improved on Mr Brindley, and is now raising a valley to the Level by seven double Water-Locks, which enable him to carry earth and stones as if down steps. When each Lock is opened it admits a loaded vessel on one side, and lets out an empty one on the other; by which means Tons of Earth are carried, and the Valley will soon rise to equal the hills around and the Navigation keeps to its level.

Samuel Smiles[9] credits Brindley with devising the special ballast boats used in the construction of the canal. These consisted of twin hulls carrying between them a hopper of triangular section with a bottom door so that the contents of the hopper could be discharged between the two hulls. Smiles writes that they discharged into the bed of the canal, which is a little misleading. It seems clear that the method employed was to build out from the limit of the completed canal two temporary and parallel wooden trunks or caissons on to which these ballast boats could be floated. The spoil could then be discharged between them. Whether this was in fact the method used may one day be proved, for the timbering supporting the caissons would have been progressively buried by spoil tipping, and it is unlikely that it was ever removed. Smiles himself lends support to this theory when, having described the use of ballast boats in the building of the Stretford embankment, he continues: 'The materials of the caissons employed in executing this part of the work were afterwards used in forming temporary locks across the valley of the Bollin, whilst the embankment was being constructed at that point by a process almost the very reverse, but of like ingenuity.'

Thus, in one easy sentence, Smiles skates over an enigma as to how the Bollin embankment was actually raised. It is easy to say that the caissons were converted into a series of shallow temporary locks down which the ballast boats were lowered before discharging their cargoes. But in that case the locks would be filled or emptied together and not alternately as described by the Altrincham correspondent. Nor would the process be the 'very reverse' of that used at Stretford. Finally there is the question of how the water released from the locks was led away so that it did not wash away the new embankment. This is only one of the mysteries of canal construction that modern industrial archaeologists must set out to solve.

James Brindley undoubtedly contributed much to the building of the Bridgewater Canal, perhaps his greatest contribution being the technique of clay puddling to render the bed of the canal watertight. This became the more vital when he had to carry canals across high watersheds where water supplies were scarce. But he also learned much from this pioneer waterway which helped to crystallize what might be called his canal engineering philosophy as revealed to this day in the many winding miles of his Midland canals. From the long fight against the 'Old Navigators' 'of the Mersey & Irwell Navigation probably stemmed Brindley's abiding prejudice against navigable rivers. On being asked by a member of a Parliamentary Committee what was the use of rivers, Brindley made the well-known rejoinder that it was to supply canals with water. In his day there were a number of good reasons for Brindley's prejudice; delays to traffic caused by flood or drought; damage to locks and other works by flood—we may be sure that the disastrous Calder & Hebble flood of 1758 did not escape Brindley's notice—and, finally, the fact that the beneficial effect of the current on traffic moving with the stream is more than offset by the extra power required when travelling upstream. This is expressed in the table at the beginning of chapter one which gives the river navigation a disadvantage of 20 tons over a canal in the load which one horse was capable of drawing.

Other canal engineers inherited Brindley's prejudice against rivers which, logical though it may have seemed at the time, in the long term proved damaging to the commercial viability of Britain's inland waterway system. While enthusiasm for canal building reached mania proportions, with rare exceptions the older river navigations escaped improvement and were, in many cases, archaic. This seriously affected those canals which connected with rivers to form a through route. An outstanding example of this was the unimproved Upper Thames Navigation from Lechlade, where the Thames Commissioners resisted heavy pressure for improvement from the Thames & Severn Canal Company to the serious prejudice of the latter's traffic. Moreover, difficulties of water supply to canal summit levels soon proved that they were by no means immune from complete stoppages in prolonged periods of drought, while traffic could also be brought to a standstill by severe frost, a condition which rarely affected river traffic. Finally, the coming of powered craft minimized the disadvantage of upstream haulage and magnified the advantages of a river navigation; namely, an assured water supply and therefore large locks capable of accepting craft of economic burden; a channel of a depth and width which enables such craft to travel freely. Consequently it is the older river navigations that have come into their own again, and a map of the waterways that are still used commercially today has virtually contracted to the shape it was before the Duke of Bridgewater, Gilbert and Brindley embarked upon their daring enterprise. The wheel has come full circle.

It seems likely that it was Gilbert rather than Brindley who was responsible for the survey of an all level route for the extension of the Duke's canal, terminating in a flight of locks descending to the Mersey at Runcorn. But Brindley took from this example his principle of constructing long levels and concentrating his locks in flights wherever possible. This had obvious advantages both for traffic operation and for ease of supervision and maintenance. He was at particular pains to ensure a long summit level since such a long level itself acted as a supply reservoir, a long pound being not so subject to rapid reduction in depth when water was drawn off through the locks at either end. Brindley, however, did not maintain this principle in the face of great expenditure on earthworks. He never constructed great embankments nor, so far as is known, did he employ the elaborate techniques for raising them that had been used by Morris on the Bollin Valley embankment. Rather would he carry his canal at natural ground level, following the contours wherever possible, securing his long level pounds in this way but at the expense of a most devious line. By surveying a contour line and choosing the shallowest and narrowest points for his valley crossings he reduced the need for heavy embanking and large aqueducts to a minimum. There are considerable aqueducts carrying the Staffordshire & Worcestershire Canal over the Trent at Great Haywood and the Trent & Mersey over the Dove near Burton on Trent, but neither of these can be compared in scale with the prototype at Barton. They consist merely of a series of squat masonry arches supporting a bank of earth and puddled clay.

Brindley used the same technique in negotiating intervening ridges of high ground. If contour cutting would not serve and he was forced to cut through them he always did so at the narrowest point, frequently preferring to tunnel rather than to go through in open cut since this reduced the amount of excavation required. He never adopted the 'cut and fill' technique of using the spoil excavated from cuttings to form adjacent embankments. Such a technique was the fruit of a later day when earth-moving methods were more highly developed and when experience had provided some knowledge of soil mechanics. A decision to use cut and fill methods must be taken at the survey stage and there is no evidence that Brindley's surveys took such a factor into consideration. Nevertheless there can be nothing but admiration for the way in which Brindley and his assistants surveyed the routes for their great cross of canals across the face of England, leaving their mark on the English landscape for all time as mute witness to their skill. For in laying out a railway or a road the levels may be adapted to possible inaccuracies in the survey, whereas in the case of a miles long level of water there is no room for mistakes.

It is manifestly impossible that Brindley, with his old mare (of which he was extravagantly fond) as his only means of transport, could have carried out the detailed surveys for, let alone actively superintended, so great a mileage of new canals. But the old craftsman had an excellent eye for suitable canal country and he would ride along the most likely canal line making what he called an 'ochilor survey' and, having made his recommendations to the company concerned and won their acceptance, he would then leave the detailed survey and construction to assistants. These assistants served him well. The best known were his pupil Robert Whitworth, his brother-in-law Hugh Henshall, and Thomas Dadford senior, so called because his two sons, Thomas and John, followed him as canal engineers. Brindley would recommend such men for employment to the company concerned and then hold a watching brief, superintending their work so far as it was practicable. Companies not infrequently complained that Mr Brindley was not giving their canal as much personal attention as he should, or as he had contracted to give.

Although they were promoted quite separately, the Acts authorizing construction of the Trent & Mersey and the Staffordshire & Worcestershire canals both received the Royal Assent on the same day, 14 May 1766. Hugh Henshall on the former and Thomas Dadford senior on the latter were appointed Brindley's deputies, Henshall succeeding as chief engineer of the Trent & Mersey on his master's death in 1772.

The Staffordshire & Worcestershire canal was planned to extend from a junction with the Trent & Mersey at Great Haywood through Penkridge and Kidderminster to the Severn at Stourport. Making use of the valleys of the rivers Penk and Stour, it had its summit level on the Trent/Severn watershed at Compton, near Wolverhampton. By the completion of these two waterways, therefore, three of the four rivers would be united. More than this, by the authorization of a short but vitally important waterway in 1768, the trade of Birmingham and the Black Country would be given direct access to the Severn. This was the Birmingham Canal from that city to Wolverhampton and so to a junction with the Staffordshire & Worcestershire's summit level at Aldersley. Robert Whitworth was appointed Brindley's deputy to the Birmingham Company, with Samuel Simcock, a less well known member of Brindley's team, as his assistant.

Where the Trent & Mersey was concerned there was some competition between the Bridgewater Canal and the Weaver Navigation as to which waterway the new canal would join. The Duke astutely won this contest by abandoning his original intention of taking his canal to join the Mersey at Hempstones and proposing a junction with the Trent & Mersey at Preston Brook, continuing from thence to Runcorn. This would mean that all Mersey-bound traffic from the Trent & Mersey would pass over his canal as well as the Manchester traffic.

The Runcorn locks on the Bridgewater canal were designed to admit the smaller 'flats' trading on the Mersey, the dimensions of their chambers being 71 ft 11 in long by 15 ft broad. At this juncture somebody, presumably James Brindley, made the crucial decision to halve the breadth dimension for the chambers of the locks on the Trent

& Mersey and its connections. In this way the standard type of lock used on the Midland canals, with a chamber measuring approximately 72 ft by 7 ft 6 in, was evolved and a special type of boat, the 'narrow boat' or 'long boat' was designed to suit them. This may have been an elongated version of the boats built for the underground canal system at Worsley, the 'starvationers' as they were called, which had to be of considerably reduced dimensions, in order to negotiate the tunnels.

Economy in the use of water from summit levels was one reason for the decision to reduce the lock dimensions, but a more important consideration was economy in money. With the example of the Bridgewater canal extension under construction before them, the proprietors of the new canals very probably decided that to build a trunk waterway across England upon such a grand scale would be impossibly expensive. For to make a waterway suitable for wide craft is not simply a question of building locks, or bridges and tunnels of appropriate dimensions; the whole of the channel must be of more generous proportions if such boats are to travel well and to pass each other freely. For it was realized even at this date that the ability of a boat to travel freely in a restricted channel depended on a generous ratio between the cross sectional area of the boat and that of the waterway. Hence the decision to adopt a design of boat which combined maximum carrying capacity in its length with minimum frontal area.

In the eighteenth century, the arguments governing such a crucial decision must have seemed unanswerable, but today the 'narrow boat', and with it the whole of the Midland narrow canal system, has become the victim of economic change; in 1966 the payload of 30 tons per boat, which must have seemed more than adequate in 1766, can no longer justify the labour expended in working them. But Brindley may be forgiven his failure to anticipate economic conditions two centuries in the future.

At this time Brindley had never built a lock, and he appears to have harboured some peculiar notions on the subject. He insisted that the Runcorn locks should have chambers of unbonded masonry and had a stubborn argument with the Duke on the subject in which, fortunately, his view did not prevail. He had not, presumably, heard of John Smeaton's use of hydraulic lime mortar for bonding the masonry of the lock chambers on the Calder & Hebble. By the time the first locks on his Midland canals were built, Brindley must have had second thoughts for their chambers were of bonded brickwork and masonry.

There is a long-standing tradition that Brindley first built an experimental lock in the grounds of Turnhurst, the old house conveniently near the summit of the Trent & Mersey canal which he bought when, at the age of forty-nine, he married Anne Henshall. Precisely why Brindley should have found it necessary to experiment with a device already proved is not clear. Perhaps it was to deterimne the best arrangement of sluices; perhaps, with the conservatism of a middle-aged craftsman, he needed to prove to his own satisfaction the merits of hydraulic lime. Be that as it may, Brindley determined the standard design of narrow canal lock and the first to be built of this type is said to have been the lock at Compton where the Staffordshire & Worcestershire Canal begins its descent to the Severn from its summit level.

Brindley adopted as his standard a single upper gate closing against a cill at right-angles to the lock walls and double mitre gates at the bottom end of the chamber. Lower gates have to extend to the bottom of the lock chamber and single gates for this purpose were doubtless rejected on account of their great weight and size. Sluices or 'paddles' raised by rack-and-pinion gearing were incorporated in all the lock gates as had become orthodox practice on river navigation locks. But in order to speed filling the lock chamber and to prevent the top gate paddles discharging over the bows of the boat when filling commenced, 'ground paddles' were provided, one on either bank at the head of the lock, which communicated with the lock chamber by underground culverts. Brindley built his lock chamber walls with a pronounced 'batter', presumably to counteract the effect of lateral pressure from the ground, particularly when frost bound.

In order to regulate the level of the water in the canal 'pounds' between locks and prevent them becoming over full, it is necessary to provide a spill weir beside each lock. The weir is constructed to one side of the upper entrance to the lock and the water is conveyed from it to the lower pound either by an underground culvert or an open leat. The weirs on the Staffordshire & Worcestershire canal are of an unusual design being built of brick in the form of a shallow tundish whose outer rim forms the cill of the weir, its centre being the mouth of the culvert. Advantages of this type of weir are that they occupy less space than a straight weir of equivalent capacity and are less likely to become fouled by floating debris, but their design was never repeated, probably because they were more costly to construct.

Apart from these unusual weirs, the Staffordshire & Worcestershire canal lock became, with minor variations, the standard for the whole of the narrow canal system of the Midlands.

Six locks below the summit lock at Compton is the first of three unusual locks at the Bratch. At this point the canal descends so abruptly into the valley of the Smestow Brook that the three locks follow one another so closely that the top gates of the first and second in the flight are only a few feet away from the lower gates of the lock next above, the miniscule pound between them being augmented by a small reservoir communicating with it by a culvert under the towing path. A more economical method of achieving the same end would have been to have made one pair of lower gates also serve as upper gates for the lock below. Brindley evidently realized this for locks 20 and 21 at Botterham, just below the Bratch, are built in this way as a 'double lock' or 'riser'. Two other examples of double locks may be seen at Stourport, leading from the basin to the River Severn. An engraving of Stourport made in 1776, however, makes it clear that the two parallel barge locks of normal pattern are the originals and that these double 'boat-locks' were built later, presumably to economize water when single narrow boats required to lock out into the river.

This conjunction of locks on the Staffordshire & Worcestershire Canal has naturally led to the assumption that it marks the origination of the double lock, but in fact Henry Berry built two double wide locks on the St Helens Canal, *c.* 1760. What is known as Old Double Lock at Blackbrook at the head of the main line of the St Helens Canal is, in origin, the oldest lock of this type in England.

When more than two lock chambers are united in this way to over-come an exceptionally steep change of level they are termed 'a stair-case', but this expedient was not employed on any of the canals associated with Brindley.

Work on the Staffordshire & Worcestershire proceeded smoothly. The canal was complete by the end of 1770 and on 14 September 1772, just a fortnight before James Brindley's death at Turnhurst at the age of fifty-six, the Birmingham Canal was linked with it by the comple-tion of the flight of twenty-one locks at Wolverhampton. As Brindley canals go, the Staffordshire & Worcestershire keeps a reasonably direct course which it follows to this day. The Birmingham, on the other hand, was extremely devious, so much so that of the present Birming-ham Canal main line the five miles from Deepfields Junction to

Aldersley is the only substantial portion of the original canal remaining. The Wednesbury Oak Loop Line from Deepfields to Bloomfield and the Old Main Loop Line from Tipton Factory to Smethwick represent sections of the old canal which were by-passed by Coseley Tunnel and other improvement works.

Trade was now free to flow from the Black Country to the Severn, and Stourport quickly became a flourishing inland port, but the key waterway in the grand design, the Trent & Mersey, was still far from complete. In 1767 Brindley maintained stoutly that the canal would be completed in five years and was prepared to stake a bet of £200 on it. But at the same time the percipient Josiah Wedgwood was writing to a friend: 'I am afraid he [Brindley] will do too much, & leave us before his vast designs are executed; he is so incessantly harassed on every side, that he hath no rest, either for his mind, or Body, & will not be prevailed upon to have proper care for his health . . .'[10] Wedgwood's forebodings proved sadly correct for Brindley died of untreated diabetes five years before the Trent & Mersey was completed.

Cutting the canal up the valley of the Trent from its junction with that river at Derwent Mouth was relatively easy and this may have encouraged Brindley to make his rash forecast. The only considerable engineering works were two aqueducts, one of twenty-three arches over the Dove near Burton, one of six arches over the Trent at Brindley's Bank, near Rugeley, and a short tunnel through rock at Armitage.* This section of the canal was completed as far as Stone in 1771 and was carried to a temporary wharf at Stoke a few days after Brindley's death. Construction of the canal line through Cheshire from the Red Bull at Lawton at the western end of the summit to Preston Brook proved much more slow and difficult, but by the end of September 1775 it had been completed as far as Middlewich, a length which includes the thirty-five locks (the 'Cheshire Locks') by which the canal descends from the Staffordshire uplands into the Cheshire Plain. In the same year the 1,239 yard tunnel under Preston-on-the-Hill was completed, enabling three miles of canal to be opened from the junction with the Bridgewater at Preston Brook to Acton Bridge Wharf. The remaining section between Middlewich and Acton proved very difficult to execute. It had originally been planned to carry the waterway along the contours of the north side of the Weaver valley, but the terrace on

* Armitage Tunnel (130 yd) has a towing path, the earliest example of its kind.

this steep slope would not hold; there were constant slips and Hugh Henshall finally resolved to tunnel. Hence the two tunnels at Barnton (572 yds) and Saltersford (424 yds). But the greatest task of all proved to be the great tunnel, 2,880 yards long, on the summit level at Harecastle by which Brindley had planned to pierce the central watershed.

Harecastle tunnel took eleven years to complete instead of the five that Brindley had estimated. This estimate had probably been based on conditions encountered in forming the underground canal system at Worsley, since this was the only precedent when work at Harecastle began. Here conditions proved very different. First a treacherous quicksand was encountered at the northern end of the tunnel, and at least one pumping engine had to be erected to deal with the influx of water. Then exceptionally hard rock, Millstone grit and Rowley Rag, was met with, which caused the miners infinite trouble. Just how heroic a struggle it was may be judged from the words of a report made to Thomas Telford by the experienced contractor who undertook to drive a second tunnel at Harecastle more than fifty years later: 'The Rock I find to be extremely hard, some of it in my opinion is much harder than ever any tunnel has been driven in before excepting the one that is executed by the side of it.'[11] But Brindley's miners toiled on and as the work progressed ventilating furnaces had to be introduced below the working shafts, as in contemporary mining practice, to rid the workings of foul air. Following the example of the Bridgewater Canal, side tunnels were driven to the workings of the Golden Hill Colliery and the water draining through them from this mine was used as the summit water supply. At length the great tunnel was completed, though its small diameter made it a serious bottleneck to traffic, and the canal was opened throughout in May 1777. Ninety-three miles long, it was the greatest civil engineering work so far built in England. On the east, the locks were built wide from Derwent Mouth to Horninglow Wharf (Burton) to enable Upper Trent barges to trade to Burton. Similarly, on the west the waterway from Preston Brook to Middlewich was of wide gauge with the object of enabling the sixty-ton Bridgewater Canal boats to reach Middlewich. But they were unable to pass through the three tunnels, a circumstance that provoked some acrimonious argument, Henshall and his staff declaring that the Duke had built bigger boats since the dimensions of the tunnels had been decided upon. Thus Preston Brook became the transhipment point.

So Mersey, Severn and Trent were united, but the fourth arm of the cross, the long line from the Trent & Mersey at Fradley to the Thames at Oxford took much longer to complete and it was not until 1790 that Oxford was reached. Not that construction involved any engineering work of a difficulty comparable with Harecastle tunnel; the long delay was due entirely to political squabbles and financial difficulties. In this, the story of the line to the Thames was a portent of things to come, for as soon as the profitability of canals was fairly proven, middle England became a Tom Tiddler's ground of rival canal companies, each jealous of their territory and intent to parry any rival who threatened to syphon off any part of their traffic, the trade in coal being the most zealously fought for. It was symptomatic that as early as 1767 there was opposition to the line to the Thames from both the companies responsible for the other three arms of the cross. Members of the Trent & Mersey committee were opposed for no clearly explicable reason; the Staffordshire & Worcestershire Company opposed because they envisaged a trade to London over their waterway developing when the proposed Thames & Severn Canal was completed and looked upon the canal line to Oxford as a rival.

However, the full story of the committee room machinations that preceded and accompanied canal construction from this time forward has been ably told by Charles Hadfield.[12] Here we are more concerned with their effect upon the ground. In this case the upshot was that the Coventry Canal Company was to be responsible for that part of the line from the Trent & Mersey at Fradley through Fazeley, near Tamworth, and Atherstone to Coventry, while the Oxford Canal Company built the remainder of the route from a junction near Coventry to Oxford. In the event, however, the Coventry Company never built the eleven miles of canal between Fradley and Fazeley. Instead it was built, half by the Trent & Mersey and half by the Birmingham Canal Company, whose Birmingham & Fazeley Canal joined the Coventry at the latter place. Subsequently, the Coventry Company exercised its option to purchase the five-and-a-half miles of canal between Fradley and Whittington Brook which had been built by the Trent & Mersey.

Further south, a protracted wrangle over toll agreements between the Coventry and Oxford Companies produced the ludicrous result that the two canals were actually built parallel and within a stone's throw of each other for over a mile before an agreed junction was reached at Longford. Sanity ultimately prevailed and this duplication was later eliminated by the formation of the present junction at Hawkesbury, but it still recalls bygone disputes by being awkwardly acute. Hawkesbury Junction also provides evidence of a rare surveying error on the part of Brindley and his team. It was intended that the two canals should be built on the same level, but the Oxford Canal proved to be nearly seven inches higher than the Coventry, necessitating the present stop lock at the junction.

Brindley made the initial surveys of both the Coventry and the Oxford Canals and these probably amounted to little more than broad suggestions for the best line, for with subsequent detailed survey work he had nothing to do. Although both companies engaged him as engineer, like others at this time they were soon complaining bitterly that he paid insufficient attention to their works. This was inevitable. Ageing and in poor health, Brindley had thrust upon him an impossible burden, and in this predicament few were prepared to be as understanding and sympathetic as Josiah Wedgwood when there were rich dividends in prospect. The Coventry Company had the temerity to sack Brindley and to engage engineers who were not members of his team. Brindley's reply to the Oxford Company's complaints was to resign, but this appears to have caused considerable consternation, for matters were hastily patched up and Brindley's assistant Samuel Simcock was appointed to carry out the detailed survey, later to be joined by Robert Whitworth on the section between Banbury and Oxford.

The Oxford Canal is the supreme surviving example of contour canal cutting. It represents Brindley's techniques of canal engineering carried to such extreme lengths as to verge on the absurd. As we shall see later, the northern section of the canal between Hawkesbury Junction and Wolfamcote was shortened by cut-offs in 1834 to reduce the original length of the line to Oxford (ninety-one miles) by nearly fourteen miles, but the memory of it survived amongst Oxford Canal boatmen whose saying it was that 'you could travel all day within sound of Brinklow clock a'strikin'.'

The canal between Napton and Banbury was never improved and remains to this day in its original state. This includes the summit level between Marston Doles and Claydon which is eleven miles long whereas the distance as the crow flies is little more than four miles. At Fenny Compton, this summit level crossed the watershed into the head of the Cherwell Valley by two tunnels, 336 yds and 452 yds long respectively, separated by a short open cutting. These tunnels were troublesome to build and even more troublesome to traffic as there was no passing room. They were opened out between 1868 and 1870 although the resulting open cutting continued to be referred to by boatmen as 'the tunnel'.

The original character of the Oxford Canal is best appreciated today from Wormleighton Hill which the canal almost encircles, like a moat. Neither the Trent & Mersey nor the Staffordshire & Worcestershire exhibit contour canal cutting carried to such lengths and there has been much speculation as to the reason for it. Samuel Simcock was responsible for the survey and it is significant that he was also responsible for surveying the old main line of the Birmingham Canal which was likewise very devious. It is also significant that when the more direct line from Banbury to Oxford was surveyed, Robert Whitworth had joined Simcock. Yet Simcock's plans would surely have been subject to Brindley's approval. There is certainly no truth in the theory that because tolls would be calculated on mileage, the Oxford Company proceeded on a 'longer-the-better' basis! Earl Spencer, who held lands at Wormleighton, proved a difficult landowner to placate, and it was said that, because Simcock's line included no lock on his property, 'the navigators will have no business to stop for any purpose, so that the apprehended Danger from the inroads of the Bargemen will be less'.[13] There is a long-standing legend in Wormleighton, however, that Earl Spencer would only consent to the canal passing through his property on condition that it served the lands of each of his tenant farmers.[14]

The Oxford Company themselves, in explaining the need for the 1834 improvements, gave three reasons for the original line, economy, the opposition of landowners, and the fact of 'the art of making Canals not being so well understood then as it now is'.[15] There may well be an element of truth in the first two reasons, but the third will hardly stand up if we bear in mind the Bridgewater Canal. It is my belief that Brindley approved Simcock's plans, because the country to be crossed, the headwaters of the Avon and the Wolds of the Oxfordshire/Warwickshire border, was more difficult than that encountered on the other arms of the cross which follow open river valleys for the greater part of their length. He would doubtless approve the summit level because it was in accordance with his precept that a long summit level was desirable since it acted as a reservoir.

Because construction of the Oxford Canal occupied such a long period some interesting variations in constructional details are apparent. Some of the gates in the flight of locks at Napton are of cast-iron with timber beams. They are of great weight and have a greater tendency to leak than timber gates, but they have proved extremely durable, though the date of their introduction is not known and the experiment was not repeated elsewhere. * On certain locks between Banbury and Oxford, single lower gates are used instead of the more usual paired mitre gates. They are necessarily of great size and consequently unwieldy. Robert Whitworth may have been responsible for their introduction. A characteristic design of timber drawbridge counter-balanced by twin beams inclined to the bridge deck appears on the southern section of the canal. Proceeding south, the first of these timber bridges was sited a little to the north of 'the tunnel' at Fenny Compton, and thereafter they occur with increasing frequency all the way to Oxford. Many serve as accommodation bridges for farmers, but others carry roads; of the former, a number have disappeared in recent years, only the low brick abutments remaining. It was usual for accommodation drawbridges to be chained and padlocked in the open position, but there was often some slack in the chain so that the wind could blow them down to a position where they menaced the cabin tops of incautious boatmen.

When the bells were rung at Oxford on 7 January 1790 to acclaim the arrival of the first of the long boats loaded with coal from the Midland collieries, they celebrated also the completion of a grand design conceived twenty-five years before by men who did not live to see their scheme fulfilled and the four rivers united.

The unassuming ease with which these first canals fit into the landscape is, perhaps, their outstanding characteristic. Their coming was unprecedented and at first they must have left scars of raw earth behind them, but today it is difficult for us to imagine how any landowner, however conservative, could have objected to their passing through his property. Especially as he was usually granted the fishing rights and the right to use a pleasure boat freely as a *douceur*. Limitations of technique and finance compelled Brindley and his engineers to build their canals with, rather than against, the grain of the landscape.

* Gates of fabricated steel were installed experimentally on some of the narrow locks on the Northampton branch of the Grand Union Canal shortly after the last war. The drawback to this type of gate is that a severe blow from a boat can twist it 'out of wind', damage which cannot be rectified.

It is because the natural landscape thus dominated them that their canals are woven as naturally into its pattern as the meanderings of a brook. All their structures, too, fit as easily into the landscape as the canal itself. This is partly because transport difficulties, combined with the need for economy, compelled them to use local materials. This was usually bricks, burnt on or near the site, since clay was the material most readily available in the Midlands, but where good building stone was available they put it to use, as on the Oxford Canal on the approach to Oxford. But their buildings enhance the landscape because they were built simply and well in what we now term the functional tradition, with no selfconscious architectural pretensions but with an eye for the good proportions that function imposed. Warehouses and lock cottages both reveal this where they survive, but unfortunately many have disappeared since the last war. The fine warehouse at Banbury, demolished to make room for a car park, or the splendid ranges of warehouses at Stourport, only one of which survives, are typical losses. Many lock cottages, too, have been razed to the ground, not because they stood in the way of any 'redevelopment' but because, when they fell empty, they would soon be destroyed by hooligans if the authorities did not pull them down. It is true to say of our canal system as a whole that it is the buildings which are most vulnerable and therefore in most urgent need of recording. Not only warehouses and lock cottages but canal maintenance workshops, canal inns and stabling are either being demolished or altered out of all recognition.

Fortunately there still remain a large number of that most characteristic feature of the canals, the typical over bridge. This design, with its delicate interplay of curves, was originated on these first canals and persisted, with minor variations, throughout the canal era. These gracefully arching bridges, spreading lock beams terracing the hill, tall trees reflected in still water, these were the contributions that James Brindley and his engineers made to the English scene.

While we appreciate these canals of the cross today for their unpretentious beauty and fitness, we should not forget their historical significance as instruments of economic and social change. Difficulties of communication had an isolating effect which we find difficult to imagine today. Consequently each river basin bred a predominantly self-sufficient regional culture of a markedly original character that became identified with the region because it had been moulded by it. Even today vestiges of this ancient regional pattern survive to remind

Flash Locks: illustration from Robertson's *Life on the Upper Thames* showing rimer and paddle type

East Anglian type staunch on the Little Ouse, from the painting by F. W. Watts

3 An early view of Leeds showing lock and cut on the Aire and Calder Navigation of 1702

4 'Ballasting' on the Upper Thames, from Robertson's *Life on the Upper Thames*

5 Bridgewater Canal: the original aqueduct at Barton shortly before its demolition

6 Trent and Mersey Canal: Harecastle tunnels in electric tug days; Brindley's original tunnel is to the right

7 Thames and Severn Canal: Thames Junction lock at Inglesham with a typical round tower lock house

8 Staffordshire and Worcestershire Canal: a typical early Brindley narrow lock near Kidderminster

9 Caledonian Canal: Kytra Lock and cottage

10 Leeds and Liverpool Canal: an unusual early photograph of Bingley 'Five Rise' taken during a stoppage showing all gates open

11 Dundas Aqueduct, Kennet and Avon Canal

MASONRY AQUEDUCTS IN RENNIE'S MONUMENTAL STYLE

12 Lune Aqueduct, Lancaster Canal

13 The prototype at Longden on Tern, Shrewsbury Canal

IRON TROUGH AQUEDUCTS

14 Telford's masterpiece at Pont Cysyllte

15 Telford's Beech House, Ellesmere, once the headquarters of the Ellesmere Canal Company

16 Brecon and Abergavenny Canal: Llanfoist Wharf

us that watersheds once possessed a far greater significance than county boundaries which are often purely arbitrary. By cutting across these ancient watershed boundaries, the first canals began that process of change which the railway and the motor car would continue upon an accelerating scale. They were the first features on the new map of an urban and industrial society that would soon obliterate the old regional and rural pattern of England.

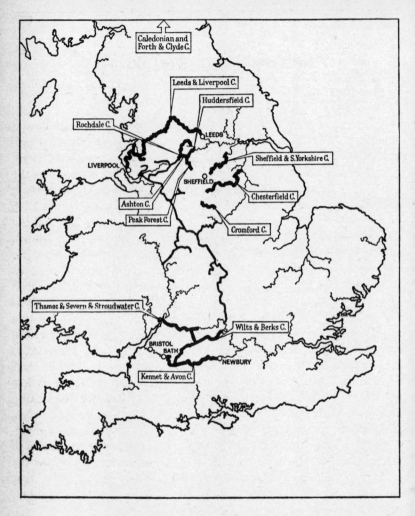

The coast to coast routes

CHAPTER FOUR

The Coast to Coast Routes

The American War of Independence and the depression which followed it temporarily halted canal expansion in 1772, discouraging new promotions and delaying completion of those canals which, like the Oxford, were already under construction. Even such trunk waterways as the canals of the cross were essentially local promotions which made them peculiarly vulnerable to changes in the economic climate. But in 1776 there were signs of a renewal of confidence, the Stourbridge and the Dudley Canals, the Loughborough Navigation and the Caldon Branch of the Trent & Mersey all being authorized in this year. Thereafter there was a gradual increase in new promotions rising to a peak between 1791 and 1794. It was this period that saw the rise to eminence of such great canal engineers as William Jessop, John Rennie, and Thomas Telford. Rennie and Telford, especially, were conscious of the fact that the canals for which they were responsible were national works of great social and economic significance. Hence they were concerned to endow them with a certain monumental quality which reveals their sign manual as surely as do the works of the great architects. It is a self-conscious quality which, with but rare exceptions, we find lacking in the work of the earlier canal engineers. This was probably because, although their work of linking the four rivers was of national significance, it was locally conceived and financed and so was not regarded in national terms. If this be true, then the growth of canals helped the emergence of a national consciousness in precisely the same way that our modern air services and radio communications are now making us world conscious.

It will help to clarify description of these canals of the middle period if we consider them geographically rather than chronologically. They fall roughly into three groups: first, the east to west coast waterways, and secondly those in the western half of England and in Wales. Neither of these groups was directly associated with, or dependent for traffic upon, the early canals of the cross. Thirdly, there are those canals which were closely connected with those of the cross either as feeder branches or as more direct routes linking one arm with another, so forming part of the Midland canal complex.

Most northerly of the east to west canals is the Caledonian which, unlike the waterways so far mentioned, was built for the benefit of coastal shipping. In the days before railways, coastal trade was as important as inland navigation but, just as the latter was subject to delays by flood or drought, so the former was often hazardous and liable to be held up by storms. A particularly bad example was the northern passage between the east and west coasts via the Pentland Firth where ships might lie stormbound for months at Stromness in Orkney. An inland passage which would obviate this long and dangerous route became highly desirable and for this the Great Glen of Scotland offered the most likely course. James Watt, of steam engine fame, surveyed a canal route through the Glen in 1773 and John Rennie prepared a second scheme in consultation with Watt in 1793, but it was not until 1803 that construction began under the direction of Thomas Telford as part of a comprehensive scheme for the improvement of the Highlands belatedly initiated by the government. It was not completed until October 1822. In the 1840s, considerable remedial works were undertaken including increasing the depth of the canal from 15 ft to 17 ft. These works were completed in May 1847.

Traffic between the western end of the Caledonian Canal and the Clyde was greatly assisted by the completion of the Crinan Canal across the Mull of Kintyre from Ardrishaig to Loch Crinan. By obviating the exposed voyage round the Mull, this nine miles long canal with fifteen locks saved a sea passage of eighty-five miles. Here again, James Watt had made the original survey, but when construction was authorized in 1793 the work was carried out by James Hollingworth under Rennie's superintendence. Later, in 1817, improvement works were put in hand by Telford with John Gibbs as his resident engineer. Though a ship canal, the dimensions of the Crinan are more restricted than the Caledonian.

Commercially the Caledonian Canal was not a success. The threat of French privateers to the British coastal traders provided an incentive for its construction, but by the time it was finished the war with France had become a memory. Again, the chief trade envisaged when construction began was timber from Memel on the Baltic to west coast ports, but before the canal could be completed the government had killed this traffic by crippling duties designed to favour Canadian timber. Over and above all this, however, was the more fundamental reason that the coming of steam power at sea and the rapid increase in the size of ships soon robbed the canal of its purpose. Apart from playing an important role in the first world war, the only long term value of the canal has been that it provides east coast fishermen with a convenient route to the west coast fishing grounds.

The limited value of the Caledonian Canal and its remote location have, throughout its history, tended to obscure the fact that it was a quite outstanding feat of engineering in its day. Priestley rightly describes it as 'one of the most magnificent inland navigations in the world' and 'one of the brightest examples of what the skill and perseverance of our engineers can accomplish'.[1] The feats of construction for which the railway builders were later to be so extravagantly acclaimed were equalled, if not surpassed, by Telford in the remote fastnesses of the Great Glen, his work unseen and unsung except by a few hardy travellers like the poet Robert Southey.

In sheer scale of excavation it is doubtful whether any single work of a similar kind in Britain surpasses the great summit cutting at Laggan between Loch Oich and Loch Lochy. Temporary railways and barrow runs operated by horse gins, all the paraphernalia that was later to be used by the railway builders, were employed in the construction of this cutting, while as soon as the excavation was deep enough it was flooded and the work continued by two of the first steam dredgers ever used. These were designed by that versatile engineer Bryan Donkin, built by the Butterley Company in Derbyshire, shipped at Gainsborough on the Trent and brought up the east coast for assembly on site.

Although the great flight of eight locks at Banavie known as 'Neptune's Staircase' is probably the most celebrated work on the canal, after the Laggan Cutting the building of the sea lock at Clachnaharry was the greatest engineering feat on the canal. Apart from about two hours before or after low water Springs, boats may enter the Caledonian Canal at any state of the tide. In order to achieve this, the site chosen for the eastern entrance lock was 400 yards beyond the shore line of the Beauly Firth where the mud was 55 ft deep. A clay embankment was built which extruded the mud by its own weight and in this clay 'apron' a piled coffer dam was constructed within which the masonry lock walls could be built.

The gates of the sea locks were built of Welsh oak to resist the action of sea water, but the gates of all the freshwater locks were of cast-iron sheathed with Memel pine. These gates, together with the ancillary cast-iron work used on the canal, came from the Butterley Ironworks in the case of the locks on the eastern side of the summit, and from John Wilkinson's Bersham Ironworks or William Hazeldine's Ironworks at Plas Kynaston on the western side. Both these works were in Denbighshire and the iron was shipped from Chester.

The use of such a canal by sailing vessels posed particular problems and to protect the lock gates from assault by craft out of control or mismanaged, chains were stretched across the lock entrances which were only to be lowered by lock keepers when they were satisfied that an approaching craft had slackened speed and was under control. Although sail has long since given way to more manoeuvrable powered craft, this practice has persisted.

Before the Caledonian Canal was even begun, another water link between the eastern and western seas had been built across the Lowlands of Scotland. This was the Forth & Clyde canal running from the Firth of Forth (Carron River) at Grangemouth to the Clyde at Bowling Harbour, a distance of thirty-five miles with thirty-nine locks. This should be compared with sixty miles and twenty-nine locks for the Caledonian Canal passage, although only twenty-one-and-a-half miles of the latter are in canal, the rest consisting of a series of freshwater lochs.

The propinquity of the Firths of Forth and Clyde invited canal proposals, and schemes for uniting them had been discussed since the time of Charles II. Nothing was done until construction was authorized by an Act of 8 March 1768 to plans and estimates prepared by John Smeaton. The Forth & Clyde was, indeed, Smeaton's greatest canal work although he was unable to see it through to completion. Work began under his direction at the eastern end and at first proceeded so rapidly that half the canal had been completed in two years and nine months after the passing of the Act. There was then a hiatus due to a disagreement between the engineer and the proprietors, but when this had been composed Smeaton continued the work to within six miles of the Clyde where it stopped for lack of funds in 1775. By the time work was restarted after an interval of nine years, Smeaton had retired from practice and the canal was completed under the direction of Robert Whitworth. It was opened throughout on 28 July 1790.

The outstanding engineering feature of the Forth & Clyde is the number of stone built aqueducts, forty-three in all, of which ten are of substantial size. The most outstanding are those over the Luggie Water at Kirkintilloch and over the Kelvin River near Maryhill, to the north-west of Glasgow. Unlike Telford, who was able to use the River Garry and its lochs as a natural feed for his canal through the Great Glen, Smeaton had to construct large reservoirs to supply his sixteen mile summit level. That at Kilmananmuir is seventy acres in extent with a depth of 22 ft at the sluice, while that at Kilsyth, which impounds streams falling from the Kilsyth hills, is of fifty acres with a depth of 24 ft.

As a sea to sea route for shipping, the Forth & Clyde was of less value, even at the time it was built, than the Caledonian on account of its more restricted dimensions. Although it was twice deepened, the ultimate depth being 10 ft, the locks limited its use to craft not exceeding 68 ft 6 in long by 19 ft 8 in beam, whereas the Caledonian Canal can pass craft 150 ft long by 35 ft beam drawing 13 ft 6 in. On the other hand, unlike the Caledonian, the Forth & Clyde enjoyed considerable local trade thanks to its position in the industrial lowlands and near the Scottish coalfields. Two of the earliest railways in Scotland, the Monkland & Kirkintilloch and the Glasgow & Garnkirk fed traffic to it until they became absorbed in a larger railway network, while there was a considerable flow of traffic from the Monkland Canal at Port Dundas via the Glasgow branch which joined the main line at the western end of the summit level.

In 1821 the Forth & Clyde was joined by another waterway. This was the Edinburgh & Glasgow Union Canal from a terminal basin at Port Hopetoun (Lothian Road), Edinburgh, to a junction with the Forth & Clyde at the sixteenth lock, two miles west of Falkirk. Although the Union Canal (as it is commonly called) was constructed by Baird, its line was surveyed by Telford and is remarkable for the fact that, with the exception of a flight of locks descending to the junction at Falkirk, it follows an unbroken level for thirty miles. Like the older waterway with which it connects, it is remarkable for its aqueducts over the Avon, Almond and Leith rivers, that over the Avon being 80 ft above the river. There is also a tunnel at Black Hill, Falkirk, 696 yards long. To supply this long high-level summit with water, reservoirs were constructed at Barbauchlay, Loch Coat and Cobbinshaw. There was also a feeder from the Almond River, three miles in length which, according to Priestley, later crossed that river by a 'suspension aqueduct' and passed through three tunnels before joining the canal.[2]

Traffic ceased on the Monkland Canal in 1934 and two years later the Union Canal locks at Falkirk were filled in, thus isolating the long summit level. This withering of the branches meant that traffic dwindled on the Forth & Clyde until by the 1950s it was only used by fishing boats making for the west coast fishing grounds or by occasional pleasure craft. It was closed in 1961. What undoubtedly hastened its end was the fact that, because it was originally planned as a sea to sea canal, all road crossings were by moving bridges to allow unlimited headroom for sailing vessels. Originally there were thirty-three drawbridges on the canal, but many of these were later replaced by single or double leaf swing bridges or, in some cases, by power operated bascule bridges. These bridges not only hampered navigation but caused an obstruction on the main roads between the Lowlands and Highlands that became more irksome as road traffic increased. To have replaced them by fixed bridges allowing adequate headroom would have been extremely costly so Smeaton's Forth & Clyde became a victim of the 'motor mania'.

In northern England the formidable barrier of the Pennines ruled out all thought of a ship canal, even one of the modest dimensions of the Forth & Clyde, and the three canals which eventually crossed the Pennines were designed purely for internal trade between the growing industrial towns of Yorkshire and Lancashire, although they also provided water links between the Humber and Mersey ports. So formidable was the Pennine barrier that before the coming of these canals, pack horse trains were the only practicable form of transport between Yorkshire and Lancashire for most of the year.

The most northerly and the oldest in origin of the three trans-Pennine water routes is the Leeds & Liverpool Canal, 127 miles long, the longest main line of canal in Britain to be controlled by one company. The originator of the project was a Mr Longbotham of Halifax, who was inspired by an inspection of the works of the Bridgewater Canal. His proposed route was resurveyed by James Brindley and Robert Whitworth, an authorizing Act was obtained in May 1770 and, since Brindley and Whitworth were too heavily committed to undertake it, Longbotham superintended the building himself, beginning simultaneously at the eastern end from a junction with the Aire & Calder Navigation at Leeds bridge and from the western end at Liverpool. At first, rapid progress was made, but owing to the difficulty of the work and shortage of capital, forty-six years would pass before the main line was finally completed. This despite the fact that the route made use of two existing waterways for part of its course, the Lancaster Canal (South End)* and the old Douglas Navigation constructed by Thomas Steers in 1742.

The history of the slow growth of this long line of canal may be summarized as follows:

Commenced	Date completed	Engineer	Section	Length m	f
1770	1777, June	Longbotham	Leeds River Lock to bottom lock, Gargrave	33	2
1790	1796, May	Whitworth	Gargrave to Burnley	21	2
1796	1801, April	Whitworth	Burnley to Enfield Wharf	7	6
1801	1810, June	Fletcher	Enfield to Blackburn	8	6
1810	1816, October	Fletcher	Blackburn to Wigan	21	4

(This section included 10 m 6 f of the Lancaster Canal south end from Johnson's Hillock top lock (Cophurst) to Wigan top lock at Kirklees.)

1783	1790c	Whitworth	Wigan to Parbold	7	0
1770	1775	Longbotham	Parbold to Liverpool, Pall Mall basin	27	6
			TOTAL	127	2

A lucrative trade soon developed on the sundered Lancashire and Yorkshire portions and this may help to account for the long delay by giving no incentive to complete the difficult central section. Indeed throughout the canal's history, trade conformed to this pattern, through trade over the summit being comparatively light.

It should be explained that in January 1772 the company bought

* See next chapter.

a controlling interest in the old Douglas Navigation and built a three-and-a-half mile branch from their canal near Newburgh which locked down 12 ft to join the Douglas and so provide access to Wigan on the one hand and the Ribble estuary on the other. Under an Act of June 1783, however, the company acquired the Douglas Navigation outright and proceeded to build a parallel canal up the Douglas valley to Wigan. A branch canal known as the Rufford Branch was also built by the company from their main line near Burscough to a junction with the tidal Douglas at Tarleton Lock, thus by-passing the Lower Douglas Navigation. When these waterways had been completed the old link with the Douglas Navigation was abandoned.

The arrangements by which, at a later date, the company was able to make use of nearly eleven miles of the Lancaster canal will be described later.

On the first Yorkshire section of the canal to be built, Longbotham engineered a most remarkable series of double locks and lock staircases in order to lift the canal out of Airedale. In sixteen miles there are three double locks and four staircases of three locks each, culminating in the remarkable five lock staircase known as Bingley Five-rise or, originally, Bingley Great Lock. Like all the locks between Leeds and Wigan, their chambers can pass craft 62 ft long by 14 ft 3 in beam. Such a concentration of wide locks is unique in Britain and Bingley Five-rise is justly celebrated as one of the outstanding features of our canal system. It must have caused even greater wonder when it was completed in 1777.

The most difficult and costly portion of the canal to construct was that between Foulridge and Enfield Wharf for which Robert Whitworth was responsible. It represents a variation from the original line proposed by Longbotham and Brindley made on Whitworth's recommendation in order to secure a longer summit level. This summit, which is 411 ft above the Aire at Leeds and 433 ft above the terminal basin at Liverpool, includes the 1,640 yard tunnel at Foulridge and the two summit reservoirs. The section also includes the 559 yard Gannow tunnel, between Burnley and Enfield, and the great Burnley embankment. This last is the most impressive work on the whole canal. Three-quarters of a mile long and over 60 ft high, this tremendous earthwork carries the canal in a majestic curve around and above the town of Burnley, presenting the canal traveller with one of the most striking industrial landscapes in Britain.

By the completion of the Leigh Branch from Wigan to Leigh in 1821, the Leeds & Liverpool was linked with the original line of the Bridgewater Canal, which was extended to meet it, and so with Manchester. Finally, in 1846, the opening of the short Stanley Dock branch with its four locks gave the canal an outlet to the Mersey at Liverpool.

Proceeding south, the next trans-Pennine route is the Rochdale Canal from the Bridgewater Canal at Castlefield, Manchester, to Smeaton's Calder & Hebble Navigation at Sowerby Bridge. Construction was authorized in the spring of 1794 and it was completed throughout in December, 1804. Whereas the first trans-Pennine railway, engineered by T. L. Gooch under the direction of George Stephenson, follows a parallel course and pierces the summit by Littleborough tunnel, the canal engineers chose to avoid tunnelling. This decision meant very heavy lockage (no less than ninety-two in thirty-two miles) and a summit only three-quarters of a mile long at a height of 438 ft above the level of the Bridgewater Canal.

Smiles credits the Rochdale to John Rennie and so does Rennie's latest biographer, Dr Cyril Boucher. Rennie certainly carried out the parliamentary survey, but there is no evidence that he played any part in the construction of the canal after the Act was passed. On the contrary, the Company's Minute Books reveal that William Jessop was asked to lay out the line and to determine the sites for the locks. He also inspected the works on several occasions during construction and so, presumably, acted as consultant. Henry Taylor and William Crosley were appointed joint engineers. William Crosley was reported dead in 1797 so the William Crosley who worked under Rennie on the Lancaster Canal and subsequently built the Macclesfield Canal (see Chapter 7) was presumably his son.[3]

The most considerable work on the canal is the masonry aqueduct of four elliptical arches over the Calder at Hebden Bridge. Much more significant historically, however, are the two adjacent stone bridges over the canal known as Gorrell's and March Barn, twenty-one miles from Sowerby Bridge, which are believed to date from 1797. Both are skew bridges, crossing the waterway at an angle of 60 degrees. Gorrell's bridge solves the structural problem created by the oblique crossing by the use in the face of the arch of very large stones, some 6 ft long, laid in courses parallel with the abutments. Its neighbour March Barn Bridge, on the other hand, is an example of true skew arch construction using winding courses.

The building of canals involved the necessity for crossing existing roads at oblique angles, thus confronting engineers with an entirely novel structural problem. It is clear that Brindley and his school of engineers evaded this problem, for there is no known example of a skew bridge on any of the canals for which they were responsible. It can often be observed how they diverted the line of either the canal or of the road in order to avoid a skew crossing. The origin of the skew bridge is a good example of the way industrial archaeology, by careful observation in the field, can enlarge and correct our knowledge of engineering history. The railway builders, too, were faced with the problem of the oblique crossing and it is clear from the way F. R. Conder writes[4] of the skew bridges on the London & Birmingham Railway that he sincerely believed that his chief, Robert Stephenson, had originated the technique. Again, Priestley[5] refers to 'that novel style of architecture . . . popularly termed a skew bridge' in connection with the bridges carrying the Knottingley–Snaith road over the Knottingley & Goole canal which was completed in July 1826. Priestley credits George Leather, the engineer of the canal, with their introduction, but it may be significant that the canal in question was projected by Rennie.

The discovery of March Barn bridge is due to Dr Cyril Boucher[6] and on the strength of it he awards the credit for pioneering the skew arch to Rennie. Certainly the conjunction of the two bridges suggests that this form of construction was first perfected on the Rochdale Canal at this time, but until more positive evidence is forthcoming, the question of whether Rennie, Jessop or possibly Crosley was responsible must remain an open one. Unfortunately, the Company's original drawings and other engineering records were destroyed by fire in 1944. Only one sketch dated 1794 survives and this is signed 'W. Jessop.'

In 1774 Sir John Ramsden was empowered to build a short canal, three-and-threequarter miles long, from the Calder & Hebble at Cooper Bridge to a terminus at King's Mill, Huddersfield. This canal included nine locks of the same gauge as those on the Calder & Hebble and it later became known as the Huddersfield Broad Canal. Meanwhile, on the western side of the Pennines, the Ashton Canal was built from a basin at Ducie Street, Manchester to Ashton-under-Lyne. The construction of the Rochdale Canal in Manchester provided the Ashton with an outlet to the Bridgewater Canal at

Castlefield. It was then realized that if the Huddersfield and Ashton canals were linked, the result would be the shortest water route between the east and west coasts. The Huddersfield Canal was promoted and authorized in 1794 to provide this link.

The Huddersfield Canal, even more than the Rochdale, reflects the optimism of the canal mania years, an optimism that could drive a canal at prodigious labour and expense through entirely unsuitable country. On a map the project may look logical, for the canal is but twenty miles long compared with the devious route of the Leeds & Liverpool. But this twenty miles consists simply of two long ladders of locks, seventy-three in number, climbing from east and west to the highest canal summit level in England, 656 ft above sea level, between Marsden and Diggle. Taking the Rochdale and Ashton canals into account, in order to reach this summit from the level of the Bridgewater Canal at Castlefield, a boat had to climb through fifty-nine locks. Moreover, having reached this summit, traffic had to be worked through the longest canal tunnel in England under Standedge.

Standedge Tunnel, 5,456 yards long, is the major work on the canal and its construction was an extremely slow and costly operation. The canal was completed from Huddersfield to the eastern end of the summit at Marsden and from Ashton to Staleybridge in 1798, but work on the tunnel dragged on interminably, Benjamin Outram, William Clowes and John Rooth being successively engineer-in-charge. Twice, in 1800 and 1806, the company had to apply to Parliament for powers to raise more capital. The tunnel was finally completed on 4 April 1811.

Apart from its great length, Standedge must have been an extremely arduous and difficult tunnel to negotiate and in this respect published data is euphemistic and misleading. Priestley quotes its dimensions as 9 ft wide and 17 ft high with a depth of water of 8 ft leaving 9 ft from the surface to the spring (sic) of the arch. De Salis states briefly: 'No towing path; boats "legged" through.' In fact, only portions of the tunnel are lined and, in those parts that are not, the rock surface is not only very rugged and rough but the dimensions vary considerably, at times narrowing to an extremely restricted 7 ft by 7 ft and at others opening out into something resembling a sizeable cavern. In such circumstances 'legging' must have been extremely difficult and it is not surprising that boatmen were allowed four hours for the job, traffic being admitted by tunnel keepers at each end at intervals of eight hours. Boatmen could measure their arduous progress by cast-iron distance plaques set in the roof every fifty yards. Working shafts were left open for ventilation and some of these shafts, which are protected by timber stagings against rock falls, are as much as 600 ft deep. This may be compared with Foulridge tunnel on the Leeds & Liverpool where the cover is never more than 60 ft deep. Probably the tunnel saw its period of greatest activity when the parallel railway tunnels were constructed on a slightly higher level. It was then used for the transport of spoil as well as for ventilation and drainage, and canal and railway tunnels are still linked by a number of cross galleries.

Of these three waterways through the Pennines, the Leeds & Liverpool Canal, first to be projected and last to be completed, proved the most successful, but as arteries for through traffic between east and west all can be said to have failed. We have already remarked that traffic on the Leeds & Liverpool tended to be heavy on the eastern and western sections and comparatively light over the summit and this trend was even more marked in the case of the Rochdale and the Huddersfield. As long ago as 1904, de Salis could write of the Rochdale[7] that 'the bulk of the trade on the canal is carried on for a few miles from both extremities. There is very little through traffic from end to end, the large number of locks to be worked making progress very slow.' Exactly the same might have been said of the Huddersfield with its long tunnel as an added handicap. It is also questionable whether, if heavy through traffic had developed over the Pennines, enough water would have been available to pass it despite the provision of summit reservoirs. However, this question of water supplies will be considered in a later chapter.

Over and above the formidable difficulty of working traffic through them, these three canals all suffered to a varying extent from a wholly unnecessary break of gauge. The Leeds & Liverpool, with a long main line built by one company, suffered least in this respect, but even here the locks on the line from Leeds to Wigan were built to a slightly enlarged Yorkshire Keel gauge, whereas the locks east of Wigan were built to suit the 72 ft long craft of the Mersey region.

The Rochdale Canal alone was built with locks to suit this western gauge. This fact inspired Priestley to write:[8]

This canal is one of the main links in the chain of inland navigation between the east and west seas, being made for vessels of
such a size as enables them to navigate in the tide-way, and to
pass between Liverpool and Hull without the expense of tran-
shipping their cargoes, thus affording great advantages to the
populous towns of Manchester, Rochdale, Halifax, Wakefield,
and others on the banks of the intermediate rivers.

Unfortunately for Priestley's through traffic pipedream, he overlooked the fact that the Rochdale depended for its outlet to the east
coast on the Calder & Hebble navigation with its 57 ft Keel locks.
This being so, the large locks on the Rochdale merely represented so
much wasted money in building them and wasted water in working
them.

The Huddersfield canal was, in this respect, the most shortsighted
of the three because it was built to the narrow canal gauge of 72 ft
by 7 ft adopted by Brindley for the Midland canals. This for no
better reason than that it was a Lancashire promotion designed to
connect with the Ashton and Peak Forest canals which had been
built to this gauge. Yet at Huddersfield it joined Sir John Ramsden's
canal which adopted the Keel gauge of 57 ft from the Calder &
Hebble with which it connected. Through traffic was therefore
limited to small boats measuring only 57 ft long by 7 ft beam.

Thus these three canals reflect the strength of a stubborn pro-
vincialism brought about by lack of communications that seems
almost inconceivable to us today. It produced a lack of uniformity
which undoubtedly hastened the eclipse of canals in face of rail and
road competition. Today both the Rochdale and Huddersfield canals
have been abandoned and only the Leeds & Liverpool survives precariously.

The Cromford and the Peak Forest Canals should be mentioned
at this point because although both were originally conceived as
local projects for the better transport of coal and limestone, both soon
became involved in schemes for through routes and, although these
never materialized, they were eventually linked by a tramway over
the High Peak.

The Cromford Canal was authorized in 1789 and completed in
1801. Fourteen miles long from Cromford Wharf to Langley Mill,
from which point the Erewash canal linked it to the Trent, it was

engineered by William Jessop with Benjamin Outram as his assistant. The principal engineering works are the 3,063 yard Butterley tunnel and two considerable masonry aqueducts, one 200 yds long and 50 ft high over the river Amber at Ambergate, and the other a single span of 80 ft across the river Derwent at Lea Wood, near the terminus of the canal in the Derwent valley. Masonry aqueducts were not Jessop's strong suit and both aqueducts caused him considerable trouble. The arch of the Lea Wood aqueduct—a considerable span for such a structure—collapsed and was rebuilt at the engineer's expense.

The canal enjoyed considerable traffic in coal and it was coal which ultimately brought about its downfall when mining subsidence caused the closure of Butterley Tunnel. In 1904 de Salis warned that the headroom figure of 8 ft 3 in could not be depended upon due to subsidence and that the brick lining of the tunnel was 'in a very indifferent condition'. Traffic through it was regulated on the same basis as Standedge, three hours being the time allowed for boats to pass.

The Peak Forest Canal, also fourteen miles long, was projected in 1794, engineered by Benjamin Outram and completed in May 1800. It runs from a junction with the Ashton Canal at Dukinfield, where it crosses the river Tame by a masonry aqueduct, to Whaley Bridge and Bugsworth where connecting tramways linked the canal to limestone quarries in Peak Forest. The outstanding feature of this canal is the magnificent masonry aqueduct, 90 ft high, which carries the waterway over the steep-sided valley of the Mersey near Marple. This is undoubtedly one of the finest masonry aqueducts in the country and it is gratifying to record that its value as an historic monument was acknowledged recently by substantial grants towards the cost of its restoration. From the southern end of this aqueduct the Marple flight of sixteen locks lifts the canal to its summit level and terminus.

From the first the Peak Forest became involved in schemes for through routes which would link it by water either with the Caldon Branch of the Trent & Mersey or with the Cromford Canal. These schemes did not materialize, but eventually the Peak Forest and the Cromford canals were linked by the Cromford & High Peak Tramway which was authorized in 1825 and was engineered by William Jessop's son, Josias. Six inclined planes lifted this tramway from

Cromford Wharf to a twelve-mile summit level on the High Peak at an altitude of 1,271 ft above the sea. The original stone-built covered dock in which freight was transhipped between canal and tramway survives at the Peak Forest terminal and is now a unique monument of its kind.

Most of the traffic on the tramway, as on the two canals, was local. It never succeeded in its aim to provide a shorter route between London, the east Midlands and Manchester although its promotion caused the Trent & Mersey company some heart burning.

An even more ambitious scheme 'the Grand Commercial Canal' would have linked by water, not only the Peak Forest and the Cromford, but also the Chesterfield Canal at Killamarsh. The latter was an early work (authorized 1771, completed 1777) begun under the superintendence of James Brindley and continued after his death by Hugh Henshall. It was built as a broad canal from the Trent at West Stockwith to Retford and thence as a narrow canal through Worksop to Chesterfield. The chief engineering work was the great summit tunnel at Norwood. This was originally 3,182 yards long until 80 yards at the eastern end fell in and was opened out. Mining subsidence caused the final collapse and closure of the tunnel in 1908.

In the south of England, two waterways were constructed to unite the Bristol Channel with the Thames. Here the watershed to be surmounted, though not so formidable in height as the Pennines, caused the canal engineers particular difficulties owing to the permeable nature of the oolite and the chalk in the escarpments of the Cotswolds and the Wiltshire Downs. These difficulties, and the loss of water so caused, were never satisfactorily overcome and will be dealt with in a later chapter.

The first of these canals to be built and the first east to west water route to be completed in England was the Thames & Severn Canal which was authorized in April 1783 and opened throughout on 19 November 1789. Before his death James Brindley had made a preliminary survey and the work was executed by his erstwhile assistant, Robert Whitworth.

It will be remembered that John Hore had produced a scheme as early as 1730 to make a canal up the valley of the Stroudwater from the Severn to Stroud, but nothing was done. In 1759 four individuals named Kemmett, Wynde, Pynock, and Bridge advanced a curious scheme for a canal without locks in order to appease the mill owners on the Stroudwater. Special cranes would tranship cargoes from boat to boat at the end of each pound. Not surprisingly, this scheme also came to nothing. Finally, a canal was constructed under an Act of 1776 from the Severn at Framilode to Wallbridge, Stroud (completed in July 1779), and this became the western terminal of the Thames & Severn Canal. Its length from its junction with the upper navigable limit of the Thames at Inglesham, near Lechlade, was twenty-eight and three-quarter miles. Despite the fact that the canal tunnels under the Cotswold scarp, there were fourteen locks rising from Inglesham and twenty-eight locks falling to Wallbridge, there being a further thirteen locks on the Stroudwater Canal falling to the Severn. The mistake made on the northern canals was avoided, for these were all broad locks, 70 ft in length designed to accommodate the smaller craft then trading on the Severn and the Upper Thames.

The Thames & Severn is distinguished for its unique round tower lockhouses of Cotswold stone, several of which survive. The brick-built tower house at Gailey on the Staffordshire & Worcestershire Canal is the only comparable example elsewhere. But the outstanding engineering feature of the Thames & Severn is the great tunnel at Sapperton, 3,808 yards long, situated on the summit level. At the time it was built it was the greatest work of its kind ever executed in this country. Priestley wrote of it: 'the arch is 15 ft wide in the clear, and 250 ft beneath the highest point of the hill, which is of hard rock, some of it so solid as to need no arch of masonry to support it; the other parts are arched above and have inverted arches in the bottom'.

In fact, the rock was by no means so solid and faultless as Priestley supposed for only 1,390 yards of the tunnel were left unlined, the remainder being walled and arched. Fissures in the rock were sealed with oak stops and the bed of the canal was lined throughout with clay except in badly fissured places where wooden trunks were constructed to carry the canal. These last gave trouble later and had to be strengthened with cross timbers, the tunnel being drained for the purpose. Many of these struts have now broken under pressure from the side walls, and the tunnel is blocked by rock falls. This, however, was not the reason for the canal's closure but occurred subsequently. A particularly interesting feature of the tunnel is the architectural treatment of the tunnel portals. The western portal is castellated and the eastern is in the classical style with engaged columns, dentil cornice, and flanking niches, each surmounted by a blind *oeil-de-boeuf*. So far as I know, these portals are the earliest examples of the monumental style in canal architecture. They are an exception to the rule that James Brindley and his school did not indulge in such celebrations, justified in this case no doubt by the exceptional magnitude of the work.

Throughout its history the Thames & Severn suffered from the primitive state of the Upper Thames Navigation where belated improvements came too late to save it. This, and an acute and chronic shortage of water on the summit level hastened its end. By 1895 it had become unnavigable and although a Trust was formed to reopen the canal and actually succeeded in doing so for three months in 1899, the water problem defeated them. The canal was then handed over to the Gloucestershire County Council, but their efforts also failed.

Construction of the most southerly of the east–west waterways, the Kennet & Avon Canal from Newbury to Bath, was authorized in 1794 and opened on 28 December 1810 with the completion of the lock flights at Devizes and Bath. It is a broad canal throughout with locks passing craft 73 ft long and 13 ft 10 in beam and was the second of John Rennie's major canal works. It is fifty-seven miles long, with seventy-nine locks, thirty-one rising to a summit level 474 ft above sea level at Savernake, near Marlborough, and forty-eight falling to Bath. The company obtained an Act in 1813 to enable them to acquire the Kennet 'Navigation and earlier, in 1797, they had bought a controlling interest in the Avon Navigation. A project they sponsored at the same time for a parallel canal down the Avon valley to Bristol may have been a device to acquire the Navigation Company's shares at a reasonable price. Thus the company gained control of the whole route from the Thames at Reading to Bristol, a distance of eighty-six and a half miles and a total of 106 locks.

On the eastern section of the canal from Newbury to the summit there is no feature of particular note. Fixed bridges are of brick, but there are also a number of wooden swing bridges which combine with the frequent locks to make progress slow and difficult. An interesting feature of these swing bridges is that they are mounted on ball bearings, the 4-in diameter cast-iron balls revolving between two races of the same material. The ball bearing is now so universally applied in mechanical engineering that it would be interesting to

F

trace its origin. On the strength of these bridges, Dr Boucher[9] claims that Rennie was one of the first engineers to use them. It would appear from the evidence of early engravings that there were swing bridges of very similar appearance on the Kennet Navigation before the construction of the canal. It may be that these were so fitted and that Rennie borrowed the idea from them, but this is pure conjecture as the present swing bridges on the Kennet are certainly replacements. In any case, it seems certain that, as Dr Boucher himself acknowledges, the ball bearing, like other mechanical inventions, originated in millwork.

On the summit level at Savernake is the Bruce tunnel, 502 yards long. This is of generous dimensions, the minimum height being 13 ft 2 in and the width 17 ft 4 in. Boats were hauled through by means of side chains fixed to the walls. The portals are of brick, the faces, in typical Rennie fashion, being elegantly curved and battered to form a horizontal arch between the abutments the better to resist the pressure of the ground above. That on the east side bears a large stone tablet carrying an inscription in Roman lettering to Thomas Bruce, Earl of Ailesbury, and his son.

This summit level, from Crofton top lock on the east side to Wootton Rivers top lock on the west, is only a mile long. There was great debate whether to secure a longer and lower summit level at the expense of a much longer tunnel, but the company made the fateful decision against this idea. Consequently the supply reservoir at Wilton is below the present summit level, an arrangement which entails the constant expense of pumping. The Crofton engine house stands above the canal and Wilton reservoir on the east side and delivers water to the summit through an open leat. It contains two beam engines which worked until recently, one the original Boulton & Watt with lifting pump which was installed in 1806 and the other a Cornish engine which replaced a second Boulton & Watt engine and which works on the usual Cornish cycle with force pump.

While we may have reservations about Rennie's ability as a canal engineer, particularly as regards water supplies, there can be no doubt at all as to the design and quality of his masonry work, and this is nowhere better displayed than on the Kennet & Avon canal as it approaches Bath. The elegant stone ballustraded overbridge near Wilcot on the fifteen mile level between Wootton Rivers and Devizes is an appropriate foretaste of things to come. At Devizes the canal leaves its long level through the Vale of Pewsey and plunges down towards the Avon Valley by a remarkable flight of twenty-nine locks. This is the most spectacular lock flight in England because the locks are broad and laid out in a straight line so that they can be seen in perspective.

Below Bradford on Avon the canal crosses the rivers Semington and Biss by stone aqueducts and then follows the steep slopes of the Avon valley to Bath, crossing and recrossing that river by two superb aqueducts of Bath stone. The smaller and simpler of the two at Avoncliff has a single elliptical main span of 60 ft flanked by two 34 ft semicircular flood arches. There is a simplified Corinthian entablature below the parapet wall. The larger Dundas Aqueduct at Limpley Stoke is more monumental, being an exercise in Roman Doric with twin pilasters flanking the 64 ft semicircular main span. Again there are two flood arches, but here they are parabolic and of only 20 ft span. The entablature is noteworthy for the exaggerated depth of the cornice. This is a feature peculiar to Rennie and its depth suggests that it cannot have been purely ornamental but may have been designed to afford the masonry below some protection from the weather. The architectural treatment of the canal and its two short tunnels as it passes through Sydney Gardens is also worth noticing because it reveals an awareness on the part of the builders that the canal could make a positive contribution to the landscape of fashionable Bath and was not something to be hidden out of sight like a sewer. Inspired perhaps by Rennie's example, I. K. Brunel adopted the same admirable philosophy when he carried his railway into Bath.

However, in the railway age this philosophy was soon lost in a pence-saving commercialism, as the Dundas Aqueduct eloquently reveals. Unfortunately Rennie, in common with many of his contemporary architects, overestimated the durability of Bath stone. The west face of the Dundas Aqueduct has weathered particularly badly and has been crassly patched with engineering blue brick by its railway owners. Rennie and Brunel would rightly have regarded this as the act of uneducated barbarians.

One further feature of the Kennet & Avon must be mentioned and this is the Claverton Pumping station designed to pump water from the Avon into the canal on the slopes of the valley above. Apart from a small feeder at Seend, below Devizes, this is the only supply to the canal west of Crofton. A leat from the Avon drives two coupled undershot waterwheels 15 ft 6 in in diameter which are connected through speed-up gearing to a crankshaft and flywheel operating two beam pumps. Unfortunately this station no longer functions as some of the wooden mortice teeth are missing from the driving gear and some of the floats from the waterwheels, but otherwise the machinery is complete and in sound condition. It dates from the opening of the canal and is quite unique. The design of the machinery has been credited to Rennie, but who built it is not known.

Before the coming of railway competition, the Kennet & Avon Canal enjoyed a modest prosperity, carrying an annual traffic of up to 300,000 tons. But, as was the case with the northern canals, the greater proportion of this trade was not carried over the summit. Had it been otherwise it is doubtful if the water would have been available to pass the traffic. For not only was the supply inadequate, but the canal suffered from leakage over the chalk in the Vale of Pewsey and, more seriously, over the oolite in the Avon Valley. Today it survives precariously and the efforts of a Trust are devoted to restoring it.

Its neighbour, the Wilts & Berks Canal, was even less fortunate. Authorized in 1795 and completed in 1810, its main line provided an alternative route from the Bristol Channel to the Thames, running from the Kennet & Avon at Semington through Melksham, Lacock, Dauntsey, Wootton Bassett, Swindon, Shivenham, Uffington, and Challow to the Thames at Abingdon, a distance of fifty-two miles. There were also branches as follows:

Pewsham to Chippenham, 2 miles.

Stanley to Calne, 3 miles.

Swindon to the Thames & Severn Canal at Latton (the North Wilts Canal), 9 miles.

Shivenham to Longcot Wharf, $\frac{1}{4}$ mile.

Grove to Wantage, 1 mile.

Robert Whitworth and his brother William were the engineers.

Traffic on this predominantly rural canal was never heavy. Perhaps its busiest period was during the construction of the main line of the Great Western Railway, but the completion of that line doomed it to extinction. In 1904, de Salis reported that 'although the canal is not officially closed, navigation throughout the whole of the system has practically ceased owing to the income being insufficient to meet the cost of maintenance'.

The history of all these east–west waterways is so similar as to prompt the question whether, in their enthusiasm for the prospect of conquering the watersheds to unite Manchester with Leeds or Bristol and Gloucester with the Thames Valley, their promoters did not greatly overestimate the freight traffic potential. They overlooked the fact that, in a small island like England, trade naturally tends to flow between industrial areas and the nearest large seaport and there is relatively little demand for coast to coast transport, particularly where a formidable highland barrier intervenes to impede the flow. Although with the coming of electric power and road transport, industry in this country is now much more widely diffused, this transport pattern still persists in some degree.

It is significant that while all these coast to coast waterways were withering away, Manchester's demand for an outlet to the sea outgrew the Bridgewater Canal and the subsequent railways and led to the building of the Manchester Ship Canal, while on the Yorkshire side the Aire & Calder Navigation from Leeds and Wakefield to its new port of Goole, as a result of progressive enlargement permitting the use of box 'compartment boats' towed in trains by tugs, became the greatest of coal carrying waterways. Similarly, in the south, Gloucester, linked to the Bristol Channel by the Berkeley Ship Canal, is today a busy inland port whereas it will soon become an archaeological exercise to trace the course of the Thames & Severn Canal or the Wilts & Berks.

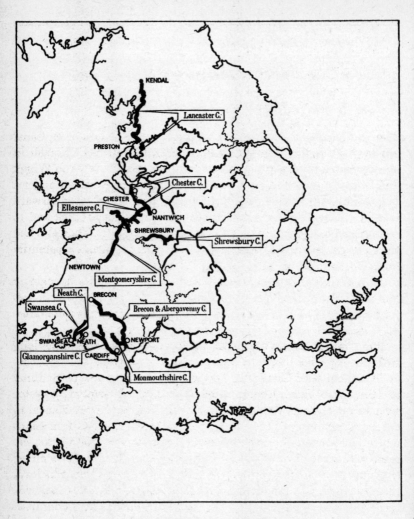

The waterways of the west

CHAPTER FIVE

The Waterways of the West

The northernmost waterway in this group is the Lancaster Canal which was originally projected in 1792 to extend from Kendal in Westmorland southwards through Lancaster and Preston to Wigan and West Houghton. Today, this may seem an improbable line for a major waterway with broad locks, but the promoters looked forward to a heavy northbound trade in coal from the Wigan area and to return traffic in stone, lime, and slate from the north. They also had their eye on the rich agricultural district of the Fylde as a potential source of traffic.

Brindley had originally commenced a survey of the canal shortly before his death, when it was completed by Whitworth, but it was constructed by John Rennie, being the first of the two major waterways on which he was engaged.

The summit level of the canal is a little under fourteen miles long from the terminal basin at Kendal to the first of the eight broad locks at Tewitfield, near Carnforth. This length includes a 380-yard tunnel at Hincaster. Three feeders supply this summit level with water from reservoirs and streams. The six miles of canal from Kendal to the northernmost of these feeders at Stainton has now been abandoned and partially infilled. From the bottom of Tewitfield locks, the canal extends to Preston on one unbroken level for forty-two miles, the longest on any single line of canal in the country. On this level there are several stone single-span aqueducts carrying the canal over the small rivers falling from the western slopes of the Pennines. That over the river Wyre is a good example of Rennie's use of the horizontal arch principle, in order to resist the pressure of the water in the channel. This section, too, includes Rennie's best canal work, his aqueduct over the Lune near Lancaster: 600 ft long, its five semicircular spans carry the canal 62 ft above the river. Completed in 1797, it is without doubt the finest and largest example of a masonry aqueduct in the country and happily its stone has proved much more durable than the Bath stone of the Avon valley aqueducts. Like the latter, the style is classical and monumental, but unlike the Dundas aqueduct, the simpler design is Rennie's own and is not based strictly on the Roman orders. Again, however, as at Dundas, though the treatment of the entablature is simplified, it includes the same exceptionally deep cornice. Tablets surmount the centre arch, that on the north side reading simply 'To Public Prosperity', while that on the south bears the date and the names of the engineer and the contractor, A. Stevens, below a Latin inscription which, in translation, reads:

> Old needs are served, far distant sites combined:
> Rivers by art to bring new wealth are joined.[1]

At Lodge Hill, seven miles south of the Lune aqueduct a branch connects the canal with Glasson Dock on the Lune estuary. Because the main line of the Lancaster was never completed as planned, this northern section remained isolated from the rest of the canal system and its only outlet is to this tidal estuary.

As originally conceived, the main line would have crossed the Ribble at Preston by an aqueduct, whence it would have risen 222 ft to Walton Summit. For this Ribble crossing, Rennie designed a masonry aqueduct of three spans, the drawings of which have been preserved, but owing to financial stringency neither this nor the flight of locks was ever built. Instead a plate tramway, four and a half miles long was constructed in substitution by William Cartwright and opened in 1803.[2] This crossed the Ribble by a wooden trestle bridge, the present bridge on the site, although it is known locally as 'the Old Tram Bridge', not being the original.

From Walton Summit, where a transhipment basin was provided and may still be seen, the canal passes through a tunnel 300 yards long and soon turns southward in the direction of West Houghton. It never reached the latter place, construction ceasing at Bark Hill, near Wigan. The Leeds & Liverpool Company originally planned to cross over the Lancaster by an aqueduct 60 ft high at Bark Hill,[3] but by arrangement between the two companies, the latter built a branch from their canal at Johnson's Hillock, three miles from Walton Summit, to join the uncompleted main line of the Leeds & Liverpool canal by seven rising locks. This branch, and the

Lancaster canal as far as Kirklees, thus became part of the main line of the Leeds & Liverpool although it remained in Lancaster Canal ownership.

On 10 September 1792 a scheme was launched in Ellesmere, with what a contemporary report calls 'a paroxysm of commercial ardour', for a canal from the Mersey at Netherpool (later to be known as Ellesmere Port) to the Severn at Shrewsbury. According to the aforementioned Report, the books were opened at noon and by sunset a million of money had been subscribed. This gives us the measure of the canal mania. An Act was obtained in the following spring, but, like many another canal company launched at this time, it was caught by the rapid inflation brought about by the war with the French and was soon struggling. Notwithstanding the fact that it included some of the finest and boldest canal works ever executed in Britain, its main line never reached either the Mersey or the Severn. Beginning nowhere and ending nowhere, it remained for many years isolated from the rest of the waterway system.

As projected, this main line was to have been fifty-six and three-quarter miles long, the route running from Ellesmere Port to Chester, climbing thence up the valley of the river Alyn to a 380 ft summit level at Poolmouth, near Wrexham. Descending from this summit, it then crossed the valleys of the Dee and Ceiriog and proceeded southwards through the Welsh Marches to Shrewsbury, with a considerable tunnel between Weston Lullingfield and Shrewsbury.

The northernmost portion of this route, the Wirral Line as it was called, from Ellesmere Port to Chester, was completed and opened to traffic in 1795. At the latter place it joined the Chester Canal, authorized in 1772 to connect the river Dee at Chester with Middlewich and Nantwich. Scenting a rival route which threatened to syphon off Preston Brook and Runcorn traffic, the powerful Bridgewater and Trent & Mersey canal interests succeeded in getting a clause inserted in the Chester Canal Act which forbade that company to build their canal within a hundred yards of the Trent & Mersey at Middlewich. Consequently only the Nantwich line was built and the canal was a commercial failure, isolated from the growing canal network, and the proprietors, clutching at any straw, must have welcomed the newcomer to Chester.

The section of the Ellesmere from Chester over the summit to the north side of the Vale of Llangollen was never built. This was unfortunate because this section would have tapped the famous iron works of Brymbo and Bersham as well as various collieries in the area. The only cutting that was ever done was a length about two miles long near Ffrwd. This was intended to be part of the proposed feeder branch from Poolmouth which would have supplied the summit with water from reservoirs in the eastern valleys of Esclusham Mountain and also served the Brymbo Ironworks. It was referred to phonetically by the Ellesmere proprietors as the Brumbo or Frood Branch.

The southern section of the main line from Weston to Shrewsbury was likewise never built, the canal terminating in a basin at Weston Wharf where warehouse, clerk's house, and erstwhile Canal Tavern now overlook the dry bed of a canal whose course is fast being obliterated. It is doubtful whether the company incurred any substantial loss of revenue through their failure to complete the canal to Shrewsbury. Navigation of the upper Severn was so uncertain that, short of considerable improvement works on the river, the prospect of any considerable through traffic developing as a result of the junction cannot have been bright. In this connection it is significant that the Shrewsbury Canal, authorized in 1793, was built expressly to provide a means more convenient than the Severn for conveying the products of the Shropshire coal and iron district round Coalbrookdale to Shrewsbury. On the other hand, where local traffic was concerned, Weston Wharf served a wide area. It is worth recalling that the links for the suspension chains of Telford's Menai Bridge were conveyed from William Hazeldine's Coleham Ironworks at Shrewsbury to Weston Wharf for shipment to the Menai.

At Lockgate Bridge at the foot of the four locks at Frankton, near Ellesmere, a branch—it might almost be called a secondary main line—led away south-westwards towards the Welsh border. This was one of the first sections to be cut because it was important to the company for two reasons: first, it connected with the Montgomeryshire Canal (authorized 1794) which was being built towards it by the Dadfords from Carreghofa and Welshpool.* The two were united in July 1797. Secondly, it tapped extensive limestone quarries

* The Montgomeryshire Canal was authorized to commence at Newtown but this was not achieved by the original company. The 'Western Branch', as it was called, from Carreghofa to Newtown was eventually built by a separate company and completed in March 1819.

at Llanymynech. These quarries were not only valuable in building the rest of the canal, but later provided a very useful source of traffic in agricultural lime on this largely rural waterway. By raising prices, the French war encouraged wheat growing and so created a demand for lime. How great this trade once was is apparent from the number of old lime kilns to be found at wharves beside the canal and its branches. There are three at Hampton Bank, two at Colemere, four at Weston and no less than eight at Quina Brook, the terminus of the Prees Branch.

From the top of the Frankton locks, a branch was extended east-wards to Ellesmere and Whitchurch, but when it became obvious that the main line was not going to be completed in its original form, the Ellesmere and Chester companies came to an agreement and the country between Whitchurch and the Chester canal was surveyed by the engineers of both companies with a view to affecting a junction. The result was the present line from Grindley Brook, near Whit-church, through Wrenbury to the Chester canal at Hurleston, two miles from Nantwich, which was opened in March 1805. Thus the uncompleted main line of the Ellesmere Canal was provided with a somewhat roundabout outlet to Ellesmere Port. But it was still unconnected to the rest of the Midlands canal system, for the Trent & Mersey company's embargo on a junction at Middlewich was stubbornly maintained until the very end of the canal era.

The junction at Hurleston brought welcome trade to the Chester Canal and Telford was called upon to restore it to order. Of its fourteen broad locks, the two at Beeston were built upon running sand and had given continual trouble owing to subsidence and leak-age. Telford overcame this difficulty by constructing new lock-chambers of cast-iron plates flanged and bolted together and tied back to piles driven behind them.

Meanwhile the section of the main line of the Ellesmere from the north side of the Dee Valley southwards to Frankton was nearing completion. On this length are situated all the major works, the two tunnels and the great aqueducts at Chirk and Pont Cysyllte for which the canal is justly celebrated. There is considerable difference of opinion as to who was responsible for these aqueducts. They are usually credited to Thomas Telford, but there are those who hold that William Jessop deserves more credit for them than historians have hitherto allowed.[4] The source of this difference lies in the fact that Jessop at the material time was principal engineer to the company, whereas Telford was appointed 'General Agent, Surveyor, Engineer, Architect, and Overlooker'. Although Telford's brief was unusually wide, it is reasonable to assume from this that he was subordinate to Jessop. It is clear, however, that the relationship between Jessop and Telford was not such as usually obtains between a chief engineer and his resident assistant on the spot, in that Telford was responsible for the designs of the two aqueducts, submitting them to Jessop for approval. Telford wrote a clear account of his part in the building of the two aqueducts in his autobiography,[5] but this is rejected by the champions of Jessop on the grounds that Telford was in his dotage when he wrote it and had forgotten the precise circumstances. As will be seen, however, this account is corroborated by letters which Telford wrote at the time. Added to this we have the undoubted fact that, great engineer though Jessop undoubtedly was, canal aqueducts were never his forte.

At the time of his appointment to the Ellesmere canal Telford was thirty-six and on the threshold of his engineering career whereas Jessop, at forty-eight, was at the height of his fame as a canal engineer. But Telford's work as Surveyor of Shropshire so impressed the Shropshire Ironmasters, Darby and Reynolds, who advocated his appointment, that he was given a free hand, subject only to guidance and advice from the more experienced Jessop.

Work on the lesser of the two aqueducts, that over the Ceiriog valley at Chirk, began in 1796 and was completed in 1801. It is ostensibly a conventional masonry aqueduct of the period although it exceeded in size even Rennie's great aqueduct over the Lune, having ten spans of 40 ft each carrying the canal at a height of 70 ft above the river. Though it was much admired and made the subject of many contemporary pictures including a watercolour by Cotman, its monumental quality derives entirely from its scale and proportions. For although Telford was a student of architecture and had architectural aspirations, his engineering work, with rare exceptions, is more austere than Rennie's. He preferred to let his works speak for themselves rather than allow himself to speak through them by adding purely architectural features. By taking the latter course we may think that Rennie sometimes erred on the side of grandiosity.

Chirk aqueduct is in fact more original in conception than it appears. In building such masonry aqueducts, the canal engineers

had from the first experienced difficulty in making the side walls
resist the weight of water and puddled clay. Rennie, in his single
span aqueducts used the principle of the horizontal arch to counter
this with good effect, as at Wyre. But on larger multispan aqueducts,
this method was not practicable and at Dundas and Lune Rennie
used iron tie rods, anchored internally in the masonry.

Further down the Welsh border, the Dadfords built two considerable masonry aqueducts at Pentre-Leylin, near Llanymynech, and
at Berriew to carry the Montgomeryshire Canal over the rivers
Vyrnwy and Rhiw. Both these structures caused the Dadfords as
much trouble as Jessop had experienced with the aqueducts on the
Cromford Canal. One span of the Vyrnwy aqueduct collapsed, while
that at Berriew gave continual trouble throughout the lifetime of the
canal. In both, iron tie rods are fitted, but here they are carried
through the masonry to external wall plates which do not improve
the appearance of the structures. Whether these tie rods were fitted
originally by the Dadfords or subsequently is not known.

At Chirk, Telford triumphantly overcame this trouble by forming
the bed of the canal of cast-iron plates bolted together and securely
bonded into the masonry on either side. These plates not only formed
a watertight bed and so obviated the need for clay puddle, thus
reducing weight, but they also constituted a continuous cross tie.

Immediately on the north side of this aqueduct is the 459 yard
Chirk tunnel. This and the shorter Whitehouses tunnel beyond it
are unusual for their date in having towpaths through them. Telford
may have derived this idea from Berwick Tunnel on the Shrewsbury Canal, since he became engineer to that waterway on the
death of Josiah Clowes, the previous engineer. Berwick tunnel is
970 yards long and was the first of such length in the country to be
equipped with a towing path. This, Priestley tells us, was constructed
of wood, cantilevered over the water on wooden bearers let into the
masonry. It was three feet wide, leaving a channel width of only
7 ft. It is said to have been built as a result of a suggestion from
William Reynolds, the Ironmaster.[6] In any case, the wooden structure disappeared in 1819 and Berwick became a 'legging' tunnel.
But this first recognition of the fact that the canal boatman should
not be a beast of burden was perpetuated by Telford at Chirk and
Whitehouses where more durable towpaths were constructed in
masonry.

The valley of the Dee, or the Vale of Llangollen as it is called, presented the most formidable barrier of all to the constructors of the Ellesmere Canal. William Jessop's original survey of the line called for two long tunnels, one 4,600 yards long, which would enable the canal to cross the Dee and the Ceiriog at low level. By the time of Telford's appointment in September 1793 this idea had been abandoned, but the line was still undecided. In January 1794 William Turner of Whitchurch produced his plan for a three-arch masonry aqueduct for the Dee crossing at Pont Cysyllte. Although on the line now proposed Jessop's long tunnels had been obviated, this aqueduct plan entailed carrying the canal down into and out of the valley by flights of locks, a wasteful and costly arrangement. At this juncture Telford persuaded the canal committee to postpone decision on Turner's aqueduct and to grant him the sum of £100 towards the cost of preparing a plan of his own. He was given until the end of March to do so, and it was obviously during this interval that the idea of a high-level crossing by means of a great iron trough aqueduct was born. Towards the end of the month, Telford paid a hurried visit to London to submit his plans for the approval of William Jessop before laying them before the committee. This original plan was for an aqueduct of seven 60 ft spans, centre to centre.

On 28 February 1795 Josiah Clowes died and Telford succeeded him as engineer of the Shrewsbury Canal. In the following March, Telford referred to this fresh appointment in a letter to his old school-master, Andrew Little at Langholm. In this he said of the canal: 'There are several Locks, two Aqueducts and a Tunnel under-ground for about half a mile. I have just recommended an Iron Aqueduct for the most considerable; it is approved and will be executed under my direction upon a principle entirely new and which I am endeavouring to establish with regard to the application of iron.'

The phrase 'which I am endeavouring to establish' clearly refers to his plan for Pont Cysyllte. Work had begun on clearing the site for the pier foundations there early in 1795, but the canal committee had been unable to make up their minds on the use of an iron trough, partly as a result of the activities of William Turner, who denounced Telford's scheme as impracticable. The significance of the proposed iron aqueduct on the Shrewsbury Canal is therefore clear.

It provided an opportunity for a small-scale experiment designed to convince the doubting Thomases and in this it was successful.

Clowes had started to build a masonry aqueduct over the river Tern at Longdon but, with the exception of the abutments, the works had been swept away in the great flood of the winter of 1794–5. Telford had reason to be grateful for this flood, for it was the replacement of the many road bridges it swept away in the Shropshire area that established his reputation as a bridge builder. An iron trough, 186 ft long, was now carried over the river between Clowes's original abutments. It was given ample intermediate support by means of a series of three triangulated cast-iron bearers resting on masonry foundations. Additional vertical cast-iron columns are carried from these foundations to support the towing path which is carried in a subsidiary trough beside the main one.

Longdon is the first considerable cast-iron aqueduct in the world,* and as such it is a monument of outstanding importance. As the Shrewsbury canal is now derelict Longdon aqueduct has stood in some jeopardy in recent years, but it is now used as an accommodation bridge by a local farmer and its future seems reasonably secure. The iron trough was cast by William Reynolds at Ketley and it is interesting to contrast the crudity of the ironwork with that of Pont Cysyllte, built only a few years later.

With the principle established at Longdon, Pont Cysyllte went ahead, but in the process Telford's original plan underwent considerable modification. First, at Jessop's suggestion, in order to reduce the weight of the ironwork, it was decided to give it more support by adding another pier to make eight spans of 53 ft instead of seven at 60 ft. Also at Jessop's suggestion, the cross-section of the masonry columns supporting the trough was increased from 6 ft by 10 ft to 7 ft by 12 ft because, said Jessop, 'I see men giddy and terrified in laying stones with such an immense depth beneath them'. Again, Telford had proposed a trough 5 ft in depth and 9 ft wide which Jessop accepted, but Telford later decided to increase the width to 11 ft 10 in and to carry the towpath *over* the trough, instead of beside it as at Longdon, forming the base of the path on iron plates

* The emphasis here is on the word considerable, for as the 'first ever' iron aqueduct Longdon is narrowly beaten by the small iron trough aqueduct at the Holmes on the Derby Canal which was completed by Benjamin Outram in February 1795. It would seem from Telford's writings that he was not aware of this.

supported by brackets and columns. This idea may well have stemmed from the wooden towpath in Berwick tunnel, and the reason for it is obvious. In so long a trough, if its width approximated too closely to that of the boats using it, the passage of the latter would tend to push the water over the sides of the trough.

Finally, the most important alteration of all was the decision to extend the aqueduct over the river meadows on the south side rather than prolong the approach embankment as first planned. Even so, this embankment is 97 ft high at tip, the greatest ever raised in Britain at that time. With this extension, the great aqueduct assumed the form in which we now see it: nineteen spans of 53 ft in a length of 1,007 ft, carrying the canal at a height of 127 ft above the river Dee. To have achieved such a high-level crossing by the then orthodox means of masonry sealed with clay puddle would have been quite impossible.

In order to lighten the weight on their foundations, the towering stone piers were built hollow with bracing cross walls from a height of 70 ft above the ground. This was instead of the more usual rubble filling which, in Telford's words, added weight but no strength. The stonework of these splendid piers is still in perfect condition.

The sections of the iron trough and the supporting iron ribs beneath them were cast by Telford's friend William Hazledine—'Merlin Hazledine' as Telford called him—at the Plas Kynaston Ironworks close to the site. Hazledine had moved thither from Coleham, inspired no doubt by the canal project. He also cast the iron bed-plates for the Chirk aqueduct and continued to furnish the ironwork for all Telford's works with the exception of the eastern half of the Caledonian Canal. The perfection of the Pont Cysyllte ironwork, particularly in contrast to the crudity of Longdon, is very evident. Telford maintained that the iron trough would not be cracked by the hardest frost, but his successors preferred not to put this claim to the test, for the aqueduct is provided with an outlet valve directly above the river through which the water can be discharged in spectacular fashion in periods of severe frost.

The aqueduct was completed and opened on 26 November 1805, as a cast-iron plaque at the foot of the pier immediately to the south of the river records. Following this opening ceremony, the company concluded their report by saying that they 'think it but justice due to Mr Telford to state that the works have been planned with great skill and science, and executed with much economy and stability, doing him, as well as those employed by him, infinite credit'. Seeing the aqueduct as it stands today we cannot but endorse this. For it is not only the greatest monument of the canal age in England; it is also one of the finest examples of civil engineering in the world and as such it is now scheduled as an ancient monument. In the 1950s the aqueduct had to be closed to pedestrians because the ironwork supporting the towpath was in a dangerous state and the original iron railings were also in need of repair. Happily these minor defects have now been made good with the aid of a Government grant and the towpath has been reopened.

In default of the building of the canal northwards from Pont Cysyllte, the company constructed a three and a quarter mile tramway from a basin near the aqueduct to collieries at Cefn and Ruabon Brook, but although this brought traffic to the canal it could not supply the water which would have been delivered from the projected summit reservoirs. Some other means had to be found to provide the uncompleted canal with an adequate supply of water. By agreement with the owner, the level of Bala Lake was raised so that, by means of a regulating weir and sluice, it became a storage reservoir. A feeder branch was constructed along the northern slopes of the Vale of Llangollen from a Dee offtake at Llantisilio to Pont Cysyllte, thus bringing Dee water to the canal. This was completed in 1808. Before the coming of the railway, this branch carried considerable local traffic to Llangollen and boats also worked as far as Pentre Felin, half a mile below the intake from the Dee, where they loaded slate from quarries at Oernant and Moel y Faen above the Horseshoe Pass. About 1852 a four and a half mile tramway was built to link these quarries with the canal at Pentre Felin. In this connection it is interesting to note that a survey made by John Duncombe in 1791 for a Mersey-Severn canal line running east of the Dee included a long feeder branch running up the Dee valley to serve these same quarries.

Today the Ellesmere canal lines south of Frankton junction, including the whole of Montgomeryshire canal, have been abandoned, and the bulldozer is rapidly obliterating all trace of some sections. But happily the line from Hurleston Junction to Llangollen and Llantisilio still exists. It owes its survival to the facts that it now acts as a supply channel for the Mid-Cheshire waterboard, and that in summer it attracts an ever increasing volume of pleasure traffic thanks to the outstanding beauty of the country through which it passes and to the sensational quality of its two great aqueducts.

To conclude this survey of western canals detached from the main waterway network of the English Midlands, some mention must be made of the canals of South Wales. There are—or were— five canals of major importance in this area, and the Dadford family or the Thomas Sheasbys, father and son, were concerned with all of them either as surveyors or engineers and sometimes as contractors. All were built with the same object—to tap the mineral wealth of the mountainous interior and its narrow valleys, conveying it down to the growing towns on the seaboard of the Bristol Channel. With one exception, they performed this function directly, following a mainly north to south route down the valleys to the sea. Where they could tap the sources of their traffic directly they did so, but where a difficult terrain made this impossible, tramroads led from canal wharves to collieries, ironworks or limestone quarries. Some of these tramroads were built by the canal companies themselves, others by individuals or groups of industrialists. At the peak of its development, South Wales possessed a tramroad network equalled only by the Tyneside area, but whereas the Tyneside tramways led directly to tidal water, in South Wales the tramways were veins leading to the arteries of the canals.

Generally speaking, these Welsh canals carried enormous tonnages and, although they are now forgotten and derelict, they continued to do so for some years after the Midland canals had begun to feel the draught of railway competition. This was partly because the railways were slow to penetrate some of the valleys and partly because, in the nineteenth-century boom years of the South Wales coal and iron industries, the demand for transport was so great that it kept both railways and canals busy. Thus the first railway proper (as opposed to a tramway) to tap a Welsh valley was the Taff Vale which competed directly with the Glamorganshire Canal. This was opened in 1841, yet ten years later the canal was carrying 287,000 tons of iron ore and iron a year as compared with 125,000 tons on rail, although the latter had the lion's share of the coal traffic.[7]

Finally, however, these canals could be said to have become the victims of their own success. For the industries they served grew so mightily by their aid that the canals could no longer cope with the traffic and we find the successors of the industrialists who had promoted them and sat on their boards promoting rival railways in order to relieve the transport situation. The South Wales canals were ill equipped to meet the challenge of railways, for the nature of the country made water transport slow and difficult. They were simply ladders of locks climbing from sea-level up the sides of the mountain valleys. Nor, by English standards, do the mere numbers of locks give a true indication of the height attained at their summit levels, for the average depth of lock was greater than in England, a ten foot fall per lock being common.

When they were built, their enginers were usually able to tap the headwaters of streams at their summit levels which must have seemed to them to ensure a more than adequate water supply at all seasons. Yet traffic grew to such unforeseen proportions that water shortage often became a problem. It was as well that the great bulk of the tonnage was moved downward, for the continuous traffic through the locks created such a current that a single horse could not haul a fully loaded boat against it.

From Swansea, Neath, Cardiff, and Newport these canals climbed inland up their respective valleys. Occasionally, where it became necessary to cross from one side of the valley to the other, a masonry aqueduct, sometimes of considerable size, would be built, but these are the only engineering works of note. All four canals were promoted and authorized between 1790 and 1794 and had been completed by 1799.

The Swansea Canal left the North Dock at Swansea and climbed by thirty-six locks in fifteen miles up the valley of the Tawe to a summit terminus at Hen Neuadd lime works, 373 ft above the sea. An aqueduct of three arches at Ystalyfera carried the canal over the river Twrch, a tributary of the Tawe. Tramways connected the canal with local collieries and lime works. The canal was also connected later to the Brecon Forest Tramway which crossed Forest Fawr to reach a terminus in the Usk Valley at Senny Bridge. The Neath & Brecon railway afterwards used part of the line of this tramway.

The Neath Canal terminated at transhipment quays on the River Neath at Neath and Giant's Grave and was later extended privately for half a mile from the latter place to iron works at Briton Ferry. It ran for thirteen miles up the valley of the Neath to a summit terminus at Abernant House, a quarter of a mile above the nineteenth lock. Short branches and tramways linked mines, iron, and copper works. At Ynysbwllog the canal was carried from the south to the north side of the valley by a five-span aqueduct.

In 1824 the Neath Canal was linked to Port Tennant, Swansea, by the eight and a half mile privately owned Tennant Canal constructed at the expense of George Tennant. In order to make a junction with the Neath Canal at Aberdulais, the Tennant canal was carried over the river Neath by an aqueduct of ten spans, 340 ft long.

The Glamorganshire or Cardiff Canal was the most important in South Wales for it provided an outlet for the ironworks in the neighbourhood of Merthyr: Dowlais, Cyfarthfa, Penydaren, and Plymouth, names famous in the history of the industrial revolution. Equally famous ironmasters were actively concerned in its promotion: Crawshay, Guest, Homphray, and Hill. In addition, ironworks and collieries in the neighbourhood of Aberdare, Dyffryn and Mountain Ash were tapped when the independently promoted Aberdare Canal, running down the Cynon valley for seven miles to join the Glamorganshire at Abercynon, was completed in 1812.

The length of the main line from the sea lock at Cardiff to the ironworks at Cyfarthfa is twenty-five and a half miles and, as the summit at Cyfarthfa is 543 ft above sea level, the rise is particularly steep. Not only are the chambers of the fifty-two locks unusually deep, but they include no less than eleven pairs of double locks and one triple staircase below Nantgarw. Such a concentration of locks is unique in Britain. The masonry aqueduct at Abercynon is also unique in that it was built wide enough to carry the Aberdare turnpike road, the canal company erecting a toll gate on it. With the closure of the canal, the present road now occupies the full width of the structure.

Immediately to the east of this aqueduct is Abercynon wharf where the most famous of the many tramroads associated with this canal terminates. This is the Penydaren Tramway which follows the opposite side of the valley on its course from the Penydaren ironworks. It was on this line that Richard Trevithick made his historic experiment with steam traction in February 1804.[8]

The Monmouthshire Canal terminated in a basin at Newport and it was not until 1818 that it was provided with an outlet to the river

Usk. From Newport the main line proceeded northwards for a mile and a half to Malpas Junction where it split into two arms of almost equal length, the westerly arm climbing by thirty-two locks in ten and a half miles up Ebbw Vale to a terminus at Crumlin, while the easterly section ascended the eastern slopes of the valley of the Afon Llwyd to a terminus at Pontnewynydd, near Pontypool, eleven miles and forty-one locks from the junction at Malpas. These summit levels were 358 ft and 447 ft above sea-level respectively. The Monmouthshire Company owned more than forty miles of tramroads to which numerous privately built tramroads were connected; indeed the company became so tramway minded that it eventually turned itself into a railway company.

The last of these Welsh waterways is of a totally different character from the rest. This is the Brecon & Abergavenny Canal. Running from west to east from Senny Bridge through Brecon and Crickhowell to Abergavenny, the Usk Valley forms the northern boundary of the South Wales massif. By building their canal along the southern slopes of this valley the promoters of the Brecon & Abergavenny hoped that by means of connecting tramways the output of the industries on the high lands at the heads of the South Wales valleys could be induced to flow northwards to join their canal instead of southwards directly to the Bristol Channel.

The canal follows the course of the Usk closely but at a considerably higher level, curving southwards with it at Abergavenny and only parting company with the river at Llanover, whence it follows a winding course along the watershed between the Usk and Avon valleys until it crosses the Avon to join the Monmouthshire Canal at Pontymoile. The portion of the latter canal between Pontymoile and the summit at Pontnewynydd, with its eleven rising locks, was cut off at Pontymoile in 1854 and partially converted into a railway so that from this time forward the two canals formed, in effect, a single main line from Brecon to Newport.

This canal, improbable though it may seem today, succeeded in its object. At Tal-y-Bont, Llangattock, Gilwern, Govilon, and Llanfoist in the Usk valley, the canal was joined by tramroads which brought the products of the ironworks of Tredegar, Ebbw Vale, Blaina, Nant-y-Glo, Beaufort, Blaina, and Blaenavon and the limestone quarries at Daren Cilau, high on the crest of the Blorenge, to the canal for shipment. Moreover, the canal was linked at Brecon by tramways to

Hay and Kington and at Llanfoist with a tramway line leading through Llanvihangel and Pontrilas to Hereford.

Today all these tramroads are gone and the line of the Monmouthshire Canal has been closed. But from Jockey's Bridge near Pontypool, just short of the aqueduct by which it crossed the Avon to a junction with the Monmouthshire at Pontymoile, the Brecon & Abergavenny remains open and there seems a fair prospect of its remaining so since not only does it act as a water supplier to the new town of Cwmbran, but most of it falls within the Brecon Beacons National Park.

This stretch of canal from Jockey's Bridge to Brecon is thirty-two and a half miles long and contains only six locks, one at Brynich, near Brecon, and five at Llangynidr. Running at a high level and isolated from the rest of the waterway system, it is unquestionably the most beautiful length of canal in Britain. The terminus at Brecon is on the north side of the Usk, but after two miles, just below the single lock at Brynich, it crosses the river by a fine stone aqueduct of four spans. A mile east of Talybont is the 375 yard Ashford tunnel and thereafter for many miles canal and river keep close company, with the canal terraced high on the wooded slopes of the valley. At Gilwern the canal crosses the deep valley of the tributary Clydach on a high embankment pierced by a single-arch aqueduct.

Walking beside these still, tree-shaded waters today it is difficult to believe that industrial South Wales is only just beyond the southern skyline of this beautiful valley; that that skyline once flared with the false sunset of furnace light, and that this canal was once busy with boats freighted with the iron of Nant-y-Glo and Beaufort.

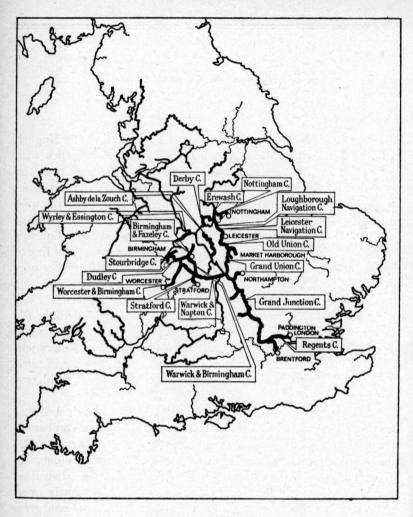

The Midlands network

CHAPTER SIX

The Midlands Network

Although the Manchester area was the birthplace of the English canal system, what might be called the centre of influence soon shifted. The great period of canal construction coincided with the growth of Birmingham as a manufacturing centre and of neighbouring south Staffordshire as the greatest coal and iron producing area in England, whose activity was such that it soon earned the name of the Black Country. As a result, Birmingham and the Black Country became the hub of the canal system. It was the original main line of the Birmingham Canal, winding right through the Black Country from Wolverhampton to Birmingham, which had fostered this development by providing cheap transport to the Severn via the Staffordshire & Worcestershire canal. Consequently its owners, the Company of Proprietors of the Birmingham Canal Navigations to give them their full title, soon came to occupy a position of dominant —and often domineering—influence in the intricate game of canal company power politics their only rival being the Trent & Mersey Company.

Another reason why the Birmingham attained such a strong position was that, in common with the other older canal companies, it had completed its line before the French wars caused rapid inflation. Consequently, while the many canal companies promoted in the mania years of the early 1790s struggled to complete their lines in face of remorselessly rising costs and were often grossly over-capitalized as a result, the proprietors of the Birmingham Canal grew immensely wealthy.

The long and complicated history of the canals in the Birmingham area has been ably told elsewhere,[1] so here only the general lines of development will be indicated. The old main line of the Birmingham canal became a central trunk from which many branches radiated to serve the needs of a rapidly expanding industrial area. But the

Birmingham canal itself was only a branch of Brindley's canals of the cross, connected to it at Aldersley Junction, and this same expansion was soon demanding other and more direct outlets to the four rivers than those provided by the 'cross'. In this situation the Birmingham Company made itself decidely unpopular. With no cloud of railway competition on the horizon it automatically opposed any scheme which threatened to divert traffic from travelling the greatest possible distance over its own canal and so earning maximum toll revenue. Any rival company that succeeded in diverting traffic despite this opposition was either bought up or else forced to pay heavy compensation tolls. At the same time the Birmingham Company added insult to injury by doing nothing to improve conditions on its own main line. Despite the golden harvest it yielded it remained tortuous, narrow and shallow, soon becoming quite inadequate for the vast tonnage of traffic carried.

The first successful canal promotions in the area to merit attention here were the Dudley and the Stourbridge Canals whose lines were closely interdependent. Dudley Castle dominates the Black Country from the summit of a limestone ridge on which the town of Dudley stands and which divides the industrial area round Stourbridge from the Black Country proper. The Dudley limestone was of great value to the local iron industry as a flux in the blast furnaces, and Lord Dudley and Ward had exploited it by working cavernous underground quarries at Castle Mill and Wren's Nest. In 1775 he began driving a short private canal, the greater part of it underground, from the old line of the Birmingham Canal at Tipton to the workings of Tipton old colliery and the Castle Mill Quarry. This canal was later extended to the Wren's Nest quarry by a tunnel 1,227 yards long. The Dudley Canal scheme was to drive a tunnel 2,942 yards long under the ridge from Park Head, on the Stourbridge side, to join Lord Dudley's canal at Castle Mill basin. From the southern end of this tunnel the new canal would fall by the Parkhead, Blowers Green and Delph locks to Black Delph. Here it would be met by the main line of the Stourbridge Canal, falling by twenty locks to a junction with the Staffordshire & Worcestershire canal at Stourton.

These two associated canals promised to be of vast benefit to the industries of the Stourbridge and Dudley area, but by the Birmingham Company they were regarded as a serious threat to the traffic over their main line to Aldersley Junction because they offered a far shorter and more convenient route to the Severn. For despite the heavy lockage, the whole line from Tipton Junction to Stourton was only nine and a half miles long as compared with twenty-three miles by the older route.

Despite the fact that the scheme had the influential support of the Dudley and Foley families, it was fiercely, and at first successfully opposed by the Birmingham, but the Acts for both canals were finally passed in 1776, though at the price of heavy compensation tolls.

Dudley tunnel proved a work of great difficulty. It was not completed until 1792, by which time a number of engineers had been engaged on it, including Thomas Dadford senior, and Josiah Clowes, the first engineer of the Shrewsbury canal. It is of extremely restricted dimensions, the height above water level being only 5 ft 9 in and the width 8 ft 5 in, so, like other long 'one way' legging tunnels, it caused considerable delays to traffic. Moreover, the introduction of powered craft did not mend matters because they had to be prohibited owing to the absence of ventilation shafts. For this reason it was superseded in 1858 by the Netherton Tunnel (see chapter seven) though it continued to be used until just after the last war.

The Dudley tunnel is undoubtedly the most remarkable monument, not only of early canal engineering, but of bygone industrial activity in the area. For at its northern end the limestone through which it is cut is riddled like a Gruyere cheese with old quarry workings. The official length of the tunnel is 3,172 yards, but not all of this is covered. Travelling by boat from Tipton, the explorer first enters part of Lord Dudley's private tunnel, passing through a small open basin from which side tunnels led to Tipton colliery and to old limestone workings. A further length of tunnel leads from this to Castle Mill Basin which resembles a flooded open quarry with near vertical sides, which in fact it is. It is here that the tunnels to Castle Mill and Wrens Nest quarries diverge to left and right. The Castle Mill tunnel soon leads into the first of two great caverns in the limestone. From the first of these Lord Dudley's tunnel to the Castle Mill quarries diverged to the left but is now blocked by roof falls; from the second, the Dudley canal tunnel proper begins. A local group has been formed to preserve this eerie industrial labyrinth.

The next canal to be considered is the Birmingham & Fazeley which has already been mentioned in chapter three in connection with the canal line to the Thames. It was planned to connect the Birmingham Canal terminus at Farmer's Bridge with the line of the uncompleted Coventry canal at Fazeley, near Tamworth. A glance at a map is sufficient to show the logic of such a proposal which was supported by the Trent & Mersey, Coventry, and Oxford companies. Nevertheless it was bitterly opposed by the Birmingham company who, finding the tide running against them, finally promoted a rival scheme. This was very properly thrown out and the Birmingham & Fazeley got its Act in 1783 amid scenes of great excitement. Thus Birmingham secured its first canal outlet to the east, affording a shorter route, not only to the Trent, but to the Thames. The Birmingham Company acted on the principle 'if you can't beat 'em, join 'em', for the two companies were amalgamated by agreement in 1784. John Smeaton was appointed engineer of the new canal which was completed and opened in 1790. It exhibits no features of particular interest if we except a pretty little ornamental footbridge near Fazeley. Two circular brick towers with castellated tops contain the spiral stairways that give access to the horizontal wooden bridge deck.

In 1790 the Birmingham Company were at last moved to make the first of a series of improvements to their canal. The short 491 ft summit level on their main line between Spon Lane and Smethwick which had long been a source of inconvenience to traders, was lowered to the 473 ft, or 'Wolverhampton Level' as it was later to be called. The result was that the three locks at Spon Lane were eliminated, making an uninterrupted level all the way to Wolverhampton, but three of the six locks at Smethwick had to be retained in order to raise the canal from the 453 ft, or 'Birmingham Level'. A reservoir at Smethwick which had been built to supply the original short summit proved inadequate to the demands of the heavy traffic and the company were forced to erect Boulton & Watt pumping engines at Spon Lane and Smethwick to return the water up the locks. With the improvement, the Spon Lane engine was no longer needed, but that at Smethwick was retained. It was one of a number employed by the company to cope with the needs of a vast traffic.

After a great struggle against the combined opposition of the Birmingham, Dudley, Stourbridge, and Staffordshire & Worcestershire canal companies, the Worcester & Birmingham canal won its

Act in 1791. The reason for this opposition is obvious—the canal promised a far more direct route to the Severn from Birmingham than those of its rivals—and victory was only won at the price of almost crippling restrictions. These included the famous (or infamous) Worcester Bar, a narrow barrier isolating the newcomer from the sacred waters of the Birmingham canal. Ostensibly this was to prevent loss of water from the Birmingham canal, but in fact, by preventing a reversal of the traffic flow on their main line, the Birmingham company ensured that they would not suffer any loss of mileage tolls. By agreement between the two companies, this barrier was eventually pierced by a stop lock in 1815, but 'Worcester Bar' or 'the Bar Lock' is perpetuated in the name of the junction, while a portion of the Bar survives as a monument to the follies of intercompany rivalries.

Caught, like all companies promoted at this time, by rising costs and fettered by the restrictions imposed upon it by others, the Worcester & Birmingham Company had a long struggle, both financial and physical, to complete its line, nor did it ever reap such rich rewards as the earlier companies enjoyed. It was a costly and difficult line to construct. The first fourteen and a half miles from Worcester Bar to Tardebigge, near Bromsgrove, were built without a lock on the Birmingham Level. On this section there are two formidable embankments at Edgbaston and Bournville and no less than four tunnels, Edgbaston (103 yds), Westhill, near King's Norton (2,750 yds), Shortwood (608 yds), and Tardebigge (568 yds). All these tunnels are of generous dimensions, the width at water level being 16 ft, because, like all the works on this section they were built in accordance with the original proposal for a broad canal throughout.

A plan to tap the headwaters of the river Arrow for water supply to this summit level provoked a dispute with mill owners on that river and to placate them the company were forced to build a large reservoir at Lower Bittal solely to supply them with compensation water. A second reservoir, known as Upper Bittal, was built to supply the canal and a pumping engine was installed to lift surplus water from one to the other, its intake being at an agreed level in the lower reservoir. The feeder to the canal from the upper reservoir was made navigable to enable coal to be boated up to the now vanished pumping station.

At Tardebigge the canal builders were faced with the same problem that the builders of the Birmingham & Gloucester Railway later confronted at Blackwell, a little farther to the west—how best to engineer the steep descent into the Severn valley. Both solutions, the Tardebigge flight of thirty locks and the Lickey incline, have become famous and both, from the traffic point of view, proved equally costly. A vertical boat lift designed by John Woodhouse was installed experimentally at Tardebigge on the site of the present summit lock, but the company finally decided in favour of narrow locks, abandoning the idea of a broad canal. Memory of this lift is perpetuated by the 14 ft fall of Tardebigge top lock, the deepest narrow lock in England.

The Tardebigge locks are followed by a further flight of twelve below Stoke Prior, the two being usually referred to by canal boatmen as 'the thirty and twelve'. Then follows a five mile level, on which a fifth tunnel, Dunhampstead (326 yds) is situated, before the final descent to the Severn begins. Altogether there are fifty-eight locks between Tardebigge and the Severn, the last two being broad to enable Severn trows to enter the canal company's Diglis Basin at Worcester. The canal was opened throughout in December 1815 and of the various engineers associated with it, Josiah Clowes is the best known.

For a long time prior to its completion, however, traffic was flowing on the long summit level of the Worcester & Birmingham, this flow being augmented by two canals which were built to join it. Despite its opposition, no sooner was the Act for the Worcester & Birmingham passed than the Dudley canal, to the fury of the Birmingham company, adopted the same 'if you can't beat 'em, join 'em' philosophy by projecting a new canal from their own, through Halesowen, to a junction with the Worcester & Birmingham at Selly Oak. By now, not unnaturally, the Birmingham company's monopolistic policy had made it decidely unpopular and, with overwhelming support from traders, the 'Dudley Canal Line No. 2' as it was called, was authorized in 1793 and completed in 1798.

The Dudley company were indefatigable moles, for not content with their previous burrowing at Dudley, their new line involved two further tunnels, one of 557 yds at Gosty Hill, near Netherton, and one of no less than 3,795 yds at Lappal, between Halesowen and Selly Oak. These were almost as restricted in size as their original

tunnel with the same consequent delays. As at Dudley, it took a
boatman four hours to leg through Lappal tunnel, but in an attempt
to speed up this laborious business an ingenious and unique device
was adopted in 1841. A stop lock and a steam pumping engine were
installed at the west end of the tunnel. With the lock closed, the
engine began pumping into the tunnel from the pound beyond the
stop lock. This induced a current through the tunnel to aid eastbound
traffic and at the same time it raised the level in the five miles of
canal between the tunnel and the junction stop lock at Selly Oak by
six inches. When the eastbound traffic had cleared the tunnel, west-
bound traffic could be similarly aided by the contrary flow of this
surplus water back through the open paddles of the stop lock. By this
method the time taken to pass through the tunnel was reduced to
three hours.[2] Lappal tunnel suffered badly from mining subsidence
throughout its history, and it was this which finally led to its closure
in 1914.

It was not only with the Worcester & Birmingham canal in mind
that the Dudley proprietors embarked upon their costly extension;
their sights were ranged on more distant targets. The Stratford canal
from a junction with the Worcester & Birmingham at King's Norton
to Stratford-on-Avon, with a branch to Warwick, was a project
already in the air and was authorized by an Act of 1793. Moreover,
this was the canal 'mania' period and although the Oxford Canal
company had tardily completed their long line to the Thames at
Oxford, there was already talk of a more direct canal route to
London. This prospect encouraged in the Dudley proprietors the rosy
dream of the mineral wealth of the Black Country flowing through
their new canal to Stratford, Warwick and points east—perhaps even
to London. At the same time the Birmingham company were driven
to nail-biting fury at the prospect of finding themselves thus neatly
by-passed as a result of that monument to their folly and greed, the
Worcester Bar. They hit back by promoting the Warwick & Birmingham canal to join their Birmingham & Fazeley line in Birmingham via the Digbeth branch. This was authorized in the same year
as the Stratford, 1793.

Notwithstanding the fact that one of its original objectives had
thus been snatched away, construction of the Stratford canal proceeded, albeit slowly. It was begun under the direction of Josiah
Clowes and the work was continued after his death by his assistants.

One mile from the junction, the 352 yd King's Norton tunnel was driven to the same generous—and optimistic—dimensions as those on the Worcester & Birmingham canal. Its western portal is of brick embellished with a circular stone plaque over the arch bearing a carved head of Shakespeare and with two vacant niches upon either side. The latter are reminiscent of those in the eastern portal of Sapperton Tunnel, and this may be no coincidence because Clowes worked as assistant to Whitworth on the building of the Thames & Severn. Here, however, the empty niches appear to be waiting forlornly for two of the Bard's better known characters to inhabit them, perhaps Hamlet or Julius Caesar.

By means of sizeable embankments over the Cole valley and at Countess Coppice, the former incorporating a single arch aqueduct over the Cole, the Stratford canal holds the Birmingham Level for eleven miles to Lapworth where it descends through nineteen locks to Kingswood. This northern section of the canal was completed in 1801 and after the usual arguments about compensation tolls and water supplies, a junction with the Warwick & Birmingham line was formed at Kingswood in May 1802. Having got thus far, the Stratford company showed a marked disinclination to proceed any farther. The failure of nebulous schemes to extend the canal eastwards from Stratford to join the Oxford having come to nothing, there was little incentive to do so and the people of Stratford began to wonder if they would ever get a canal at all. They might not have done so had it not been for the enthusiasm and energy of that remarkable character William James, the so-called 'Father of Railways'.

James had a vision of Stratford becoming an important transport centre. Besides a meeting place of canal and river (he had an interest in the Upper Avon Navigation) it was to be the northern terminus of his ambitious scheme for a railway to London (Paddington) with branches to Coventry and Cheltenham. These visions never materialized, for only the first link in the railway, the Stratford & Moreton Tramway, was ever built, while the Upper Avon Navigation was too tortuous and difficult to make it a serious competitor as part of a through route from the Midlands to the Severn. Nevertheless, but for these dreams, the Stratford canal might never have reached its objective.

The southern section of the canal is thirteen miles long and falls by thirty-six locks to the Avon at Stratford, the last being a barge lock. Construction began in 1812 and the canal was opened throughout in June 1816. Because it is so much later in date, it exhibits a number of features of interest not to be found on the older northern section. Most notable are the cast iron aqueducts at Yarningale, Wooton Wawen, and Bearley (the Edstone Aqueduct). The last named, though of no great height, is second only in length to Pont Cysyllte. The towpath, however, is not carried over the water as on the latter, but beside the trough as at Longdon. Edstone aqueduct exhibits one unique feature. When the Bearley & Alcester branch of the Great Western Railway was built beneath it, that railway company, who by then owned the Stratford Canal, adapted the aqueduct as a convenient means of supplying the branch locomotives with water by fitting a pipe and stop valve into the side of the iron trough.

Other features of this canal are the unusual lock houses with barrel roofs, the first of which is at Kingswood, and the overbridges. These support the roadway on cast-iron brackets cantilevered out from the brick abutments so as to leave a gap wide enough to allow a boat's towline to fall between them. In this way the need to build a towpath beneath the bridge was avoided. It is pleasing to record that the southern section of this canal has been restored and is now owned by the National Trust.

The large summit reservoirs known as Earlswood Lakes which supply the whole canal with water were authorized in 1815. The Warwick & Birmingham canal won the title to a lock full of water from the Stratford for every boat passing through the junction at Kingswood, and the falling lock on the connecting branch was built for this reason. The stop lock at King's Norton Junction is, unusually, fitted with guillotine gates because the fall might be in either direction depending on the level in the two canals. Of recent years, however, the two canals have been maintained at the same level and the gates remain permanently open.

To the north-west of the Black Country the Wyrley & Essington canal was promoted and authorized in 1792 from a junction with the Birmingham canal at Horseley Fields, near Wolverhampton, with the object of serving the Cannock Chase coalfield. It was progressively extended with the later development of coal working on the Chase. However, the canal acquired a more than local significance in 1797 when there was opened an extension of its main line fifteen and a half miles long, from Birchills Junction falling by way of the thirty Ogley locks to join the Coventry Canal at Huddlesford, near Lichfield. This gave the canal network in the Black Country a much more direct communication with the Trent and the north-east via Fradley Junction and the Trent & Mersey. For once, the Birmingham Company offered no opposition to this project since it promised additional traffic for their main line.

Meanwhile a crucially important event had taken place to the south-east which was destined to change the balance of power of the older canal companies and affect the flow of traffic over the whole of the Midlands canal system. This was the authorization, in 1793, of the Grand Junction Canal, a broad waterway from the Thames at Brentford to the Oxford canal at Braunston, with branches to Northampton and Buckingham. Additional branches to Paddington and to Aylesbury were authorized in the next two years. It was the biggest canal project that had been launched in England, for its long main line from London would have to be carried over two summit levels, the Chiltern chalk near Tring and the Northamptonshire oolite at Braunston, but it also promised a great reward in traffic, being no less than sixty-four miles shorter than the Oxford canal route to London via the Thames. The only waterway to suffer as a result of this scheme was the Oxford and their countermeasure was to promote, unsuccessfully, a rival route to London leaving their own canal at Hampton Gay, six miles north of Oxford.

William Jessop was appointed principal engineer with James Barnes, who had made the first survey, as resident engineer. Compared with most of the canals of this period, the Grand Junction was built with remarkable speed, but three works occasioned particular difficulty. These were the long embankment and aqueduct across the valley of the Ouse at Wolverton and the two long tunnels through the Northamptonshire oolite at Braunston (2,042 yds) on the Braunston summit level, and at Blisworth (3,056 yds) between the village of that name and Stoke Bruerne.

The Ouse at Wolverton was originally crossed on the level, but owing to the risk of floods holding up traffic, Barnes's recommendation of an alternative high-level route was accepted. On a January night in 1806, however, owing to faulty work on the part of the local contractor, the embankment blew out, greatly to the alarm of the local inhabitants. Two years later, the three-arch aqueduct over the Ouse, which William Jessop had designed, collapsed, thus proving once again that aqueducts were not that engineer's *métier*. A temporary wooden trunk across the breach was installed to keep traffic moving until the present iron trough aqueduct, cast by the Ketley Bank Ironworks in Shropshire, was installed in 1811. Traces of the original locks and the pier bases of Jessop's ill fated aqueduct may still be seen. Fenny Stratford lock at the south end of this embankment has a fall to the embankment of a mere eighteen inches. Priestley states[3] that this was due to an error in the levels, and this legend has persisted on the canal with the dramatic embroidery that the surveyor responsible for the mistake drowned himself in the canal. A truer though more prosaic explanation is that the lock had to be built because of difficulty in maintaining the water in the new section over the embankment up to its designed level.[4]

For a distance of 320 yds, Braunston tunnel had to be driven through a quicksand, an unexpected hazard which foreshadowed Robert Stephenson's later difficulties at Kilsby and which cost the company an extra £5,000. Jessop also had to report that the sub-engineer in charge and the contractor had between them made a serious mistake and had got off the correct line, an error which accounts for the dogleg towards the southern end of the tunnel.

Notwithstanding these difficulties, Braunston tunnel was completed in June 1796, but Blisworth proved a much tougher proposition, chiefly owing to the treacherous nature of the strata which consisted of rotten oolite and heavy clays containing powerful springs of water. The difficulties were so great that work came to a standstill in 1795 and, in the following January, Jessop recommended carrying the canal over the ridge by locks. Faced with this counsel of despair, the company called in Whitworth and Rennie to advise them on the tunnel. They recommended driving a new line on a diagonal intersecting the old one and the provision of a heading below tunnel level to carry off the water. Again, Robert Stephenson encountered similar difficulties in excavating the Blisworth cutting for the London & Birmingham railway.

On Jessop's recommendation, a double line of plate tramway was laid over Blisworth hill from a wharf below the present locks at Stoke Bruerne to Blisworth wharf. This was constructed by Benjamin Outram using tramplates cast at the Butterley ironworks.[5] In

September 1800 the southern section of the canal from Brentford to Stoke Bruerne was completed, and, as the northern section from Braunston to Blisworth had been finished since 1796, the tramroad served to keep traffic moving until the tunnel was completed in 1805. The tramplates were then lifted and relaid between Gayton and Northampton where they served until the present branch canal to Northampton was completed in 1815. By this branch the Grand Junction was connected to the river Nene, but plans to link it to the Great Ouse at Bedford by an extension of the branch to Newport Pagnell (later converted to a railway) never materialized.

To supply the Grand Junction's two summit levels with water, extensive reservoirs were built in the vicinity of Tring and Daventry. Even so, beam pumping engines were needed at both summits to pump back the lockage water. The supply on Tring summit was augmented by a navigable feeder nearly seven miles long known as the Wendover Arm. The beam pumps are now gone and the Wendover Arm is disused.

The importance of linking the Birmingham area directly with the Grand Junction was appreciated from the outset. An extension of the Warwick & Birmingham Canal was the obvious answer and in 1794 construction of the Warwick & Braunston Canal was authorized. This would have cut out the Oxford Canal altogether where through traffic between Birmingham and London was concerned and it was largely as a result of pressure from the Oxford Company that Napton was substituted for Braunston as the junction point. This meant that through traffic would pass over five miles of the Oxford Canal between Napton and Braunston and the high tolls levied on this short length later became a bone of contention.

The whole of the canal line from Birmingham to Napton was opened in 1800. Apart from the 433 yard tunnel at Shrewley and the three-arch masonry aqueduct over the Avon at Warwick, there were no works of note, but the lockage was extremely heavy due to the need to descend into the Avon valley. There are no less than fifty-nine locks between Birmingham and Napton; moreover, despite pressure from the Grand Junction company, these were built narrow, although Shrewley tunnel and the overbridges were built to broad canal dimensions.

We must turn now to the East Midlands where the group of waterways radiating from the Upper Trent, in most of which William

Jessop had been concerned, sought some more direct outlet to the south than the roundabout route provided by the Trent & Mersey, Coventry and Oxford canals. The first of these was the River Soar, or Loughborough Navigation as it was called, which was destined to become the first link in the new line to the south and one of the rare examples of a major river that was first made navigable in the canal era. An Act authorizing the work was passed in 1766 and Brindley was called in to advise. True to his policy, he recommended a canal up the Soar valley, but because the Act did not empower the proprietors to cut a canal, nothing was done until 1778 when a fresh Act was obtained and work commenced. Brindley's advice was ignored, the river being made navigable by means of six broad locks, a cut one and a half miles long giving access to Loughborough. This work was completed in 1780.

Meanwhile the Erewash Canal, designed to tap the Erewash valley coalfield, had also been completed with remarkable speed. Authorized in 1777, by the end of 1779 the eleven and three-quarter miles from Langley Mill, falling by fourteen broad locks to the Trent, was opened for traffic. This meant that boats carrying Derbyshire coal could now trade to Loughborough where the coal was distributed by land carriage to Leicester. The junction of this canal with the Trent is almost exactly opposite the mouth of the Soar and a ferry, which continued in use into the present century, was introduced to take boat horses across the Trent. Later, as we noted in chapter four, Jessop's Cromford Canal formed an extension of the Erewash into the Derbyshire Peak district.

The Derby Canal (1793–96) ran from the Erewash canal at Sandiacre to Derby where it crossed the river Derwent on the level at the head of a weir and continued thence to a junction with the Trent & Mersey canal at Swarkeston a distance of fourteen and a half miles. Apart from serving Derby, this canal formed a more convenient route for through traffic between the Trent & Mersey and Erewash canals than that via the Trent.

The Nottingham Canal (1792–96) had a main line of the same length as the Derby, extending from a junction with the river Trent at Nottingham to the Cromford canal near its junction with the Erewash at Langley Mill. It provided a much more direct route for coal traffic to Nottingham than that via the Erewash canal and the Trent and for this reason it was opposed unsuccessfully by the

Erewash company. The navigation of the Trent from the mouth of the Soar downstream to Nottingham was notoriously difficult, but it was greatly improved at this time by the construction of the Cranfleet cut and lock and the Beeston Cut from the river at Beeston to the Nottingham Canal at Lenton Chain. That portion of the Nottingham canal from Lenton Chain to Trent Lock, Nottingham thus became part of a Trent 'by-pass'. Under pressure from the canal companies, the navigation of the Trent was further improved at this time, certain notorious gravel shoals being removed by dredging.

All these improvements in wateway communications greatly stimulated industrial growth, particularly in the coal trade, in the Derby and Nottingham area and it is not surprising that from 1785 onwards pressure built up for the extension of the Soar Navigation to Leicester. This extension, the Leicester Navigation, was authorized in 1791 and completed four years later. Although sometimes referred to as a canal, it was essentially a river navigation, though there were extensive artificial cuts. Because their construction involved the expenditure of comparatively little capital and carried heavy traffic, both the Loughborough and Leicester Navigations were for a time extremely prosperous. It was the construction by George Stephenson of the Leicester & Swannington Railway, bringing Leicestershire coal to the city, which brought to an end the golden years of the waterborne trade in Derbyshire coal.

The Leicester Navigation had originally planned to tap the coal and lime resources of the Charnwood Forest area of Leicestershire by a canal from Loughborough. As built, this consisted of an isolated stretch of canal between two tramways, but it was unsuccessful and short lived[6] and it was in the opposite direction that Leicestershire coal was first provided with a transport outlet by the Ashby-de-la Zouch canal and its associated tramways.

The Ashby canal was surveyed and engineered by Robert Whitworth and his son, Robert Junior. It was originally intended to run from the Coventry Canal at Marston to the Upper Trent below Burton, thus not only affording a direct outlet for Leicestershire coal to the Trent but a shorter route between the East Midlands and the south. In promise of this, the Derby canal company were persuaded to extend the western arm of their main line from its junction with the Trent & Mersey at Swarkeston to the Trent. The Ashby canal was authorized in 1794, but by the time the main line had been

completed to Ashby (Moira) the money ran out and it was finally
decided in 1798 to abandon the plan to extend the canal to the Trent
and to substitute tramways for the intended branch canals to
quarries and collieries. So the Ashby Canal became, in effect, a long
branch of the Coventry Canal, winding for thirty miles through the
midland plain with no lock and only one short tunnel at Snarestone
(250 yds). As a result of colliery subsidence at its northern end, its
length has now been reduced by about six miles.

With the failure of the Ashby company to complete its line, East
Midland hopes for a direct water route to the south centred on the
Leicestershire & Northamptonshire Union Canal, later referred to
as the 'Old Union'. This had been authorized in 1793, the same year
as the Grand Junction, and was intended to run from the River Soar
at Leicester to the Nene at Northampton, where it would be joined
by the proposed Northampton Branch of the Grand Junction. In the
enthusiasm of the mania period, there was even talk of extending
the canal to the Great Ouse at Bedford. These bright hopes were to
be short-lived. Work began at the Leicester end but, after building
seventeen miles of canal including twenty-four broad locks and a
tunnel half a mile long at Saddington, the project petered out at
Debdale Wharf, one mile to the north of Foxton. Had things proceeded according to plan there was to have been a five and three-
quarter mile branch to Market Harborough from Foxton, the main
line heading south through a tunnel from the junction.

Goods were conveyed by road from Debdale Wharf to Market
Harborough while the difficult country ahead was surveyed and
resurveyed, both Barnes and Telford submitting plans, the target
now being the Grand Junction canal at Norton, near Long Buckby,
close to the east end of Braunston Tunnel. But all that the hard-
pressed company could manage was the extension of their canal by six
and three-quarter miles to a terminal basin at Market Harborough,
a work which they completed in 1809. Having done this, they
decided to rest on their modest laurels and it was left to the Grand
Junction company to take the initiative by promoting the final link,
the Grand Union Canal, authorized in 1810.

One of the Grand Junction's engineers, Benjamin Bevan, was
appointed engineer to the Grand Union and his first task was the
invidious one of reconciling the various conflicting routes for the
canal that had been advanced over the years of delay. It was he who

finally decided upon the present line. Work began at Foxton where, instead of the tunnel which the Old Union company had originally proposed, the Grand Union climbs steeply and spectacularly to its summit level by two staircases of five locks each, the greatest lock staircase in England. There follows a summit level, twenty-one miles long, to Watford including two long tunnels at Husbands Bosworth (1,166 yds) and Crick (1,528 yds). The latter was originally planned on a line to the west of Crick village, but in sinking the shafts quicksands were encountered and Bevan wisely decided to abandon the works and to drive the tunnel on a new alignment passing to the east of the village. As his own letters reveal, Robert Stephenson planned to tunnel through this ridge on Bevan's original line but, on hearing of the canal builder's experience, thought it prudent to switch to a new alignment for his railway tunnel nearer Kilsby.[7] Had he also heard about Jessop's encounter with quicksands at Braunston, still further to the south, he might have been less sanguine of the success of this avoiding action.

With the exception of these two tunnels and an embankment with aqueduct across the Avon valley near North Kilworth Wharf, the summit level of the Grand Union avoids earthworks, following a line a little above the 400 ft contour on the western slope of the Naseby Wolds. In this it resembles the canals of an earlier day, being the latest example of a devious contour canal in England. But if the canal is reminiscent of the past in this respect, in the construction of the tunnels it looked forward to the future. For they were built by the contractors, Messrs Pritchard and Hoof of King's Norton who, in the scale of their activities and in the efficiency and speed of their work anticipated the great contractors whom the railway age would bring to fame. Hincaster tunnel on the Lancaster Canal had been their 'prentice work and they would follow their work on the Grand Union tunnels with similar contracts for the Regents Canal tunnels, for the great Strood tunnel on the Thames & Medway Canal and, finally, for Telford's new tunnel at Harecastle.

A feeder up the Avon valley, once navigable to Welford Wharf, supplies the Grand Union with water from reservoirs on Naseby Wolds. It descends from its long summit level by four single locks and a staircase of four at Watford and thence continues for two miles on the level to a junction with the main line of the Grand Junction at Norton, near Long Buckby. When it was opened throughout in 1814 the East Midlands were at last provided with a direct water route to London.

Because the waterways of the East Midlands, including the Old Union, were all built with broad locks in the expectation that wide Upper Trent boats would use them, and the Grand Junction was also built to the broad gauge with barge traffic in mind, it may appear remarkable that the locks at Foxton and Watford were constructed to narrow canal dimensions. This is the more surprising in view of the fact that the Grand Union was sponsored by Grand Junction interests which had earlier cherished schemes for broad routes to Manchester. Tunnels and bridges on the Grand Union, moreover, were built to broad canal dimensions. The answer is that experience had convinced the Grand Junction company that for various reasons, most notably the passing difficulty, particularly in tunnels, the narrow boat was the most suitable type of craft.

One more important waterway remained to be built before the threat of railways appeared over the horizon. This was the Regent's Canal running in a great arc through northern London from a junction with the Paddington branch of the Grand Junction at Harrow Road Bridge to Limehouse. It was authorized in 1812. The main line is eight and a half miles long with twelve paired broad locks (i.e. side by side) falling to an extensive dock at Limehouse from which ship and barge locks gave access to the tidal Thames. There are two tunnels, Maida Hill (272 yds) and Islington (960 yds). Below the City Road locks, east of Islington tunnel, the City Road Basin was built which largely superseded the old terminus of the Grand Junction at Paddington Basin as a centre for London traffic.

With the opening of the Regents Canal in 1820, the Midlands canal network was linked directly to London's dockland and the great period of canal construction came to an end. For a few more golden years, waterways would enjoy a monopoly of goods transport in an expanding industrial society. The shareholders of the older canal companies continued to enjoy a rich harvest, while even the later comers which had had to struggle to complete their lines began to pay their first small dividends and looked forward to an equally golden future. Such dreams of unending prosperity were soon to be rudely shattered.

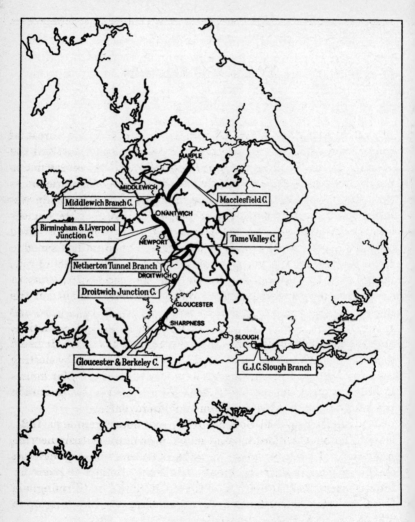

The last canals

CHAPTER SEVEN

The Last Canals

It was in 1825 that the canal companies awoke to the threat of competition from the new railways. This was the year that saw the opening of the Stockton & Darlington Railway. But it was not so much this purely local project that alerted the canal proprietors as the activities of George Stephenson and Son. This partnership was formed at the same time as Robert Stephenson and Co., the pioneer locomotive building firm of Newcastle, with which it is often confused. In fact it was a parallel but separate organization formed to carry out surveys and to supervise construction of new lines of railway. In 1825 George Stephenson and Son organized teams of surveyors and surveyed railway routes between London and the north, London and South Wales, Liverpool and Birmingham, and Liverpool and Manchester. All this activity proved overambitious and premature, for only the last named scheme bore fruit. It had a more immediate impact on canal than on railway history by alerting canal interests and persuading them to take steps to set their houses in order to meet the coming danger. Thus there was set in motion the last phase of canal construction and improvement.

William Jessop had died in 1814, and John Rennie in 1821, leaving Thomas Telford the undisputed head of the civil engineering profession. It was to him, therefore, that the canal proprietors chiefly turned in this emergency. He found plenty of room for improvement. Asked to examine the main line of the Birmingham Canal, still the hub of the canal system and passing anything up to 200 boats a day, Telford reported:

'I found . . . a canal little better than a crooked ditch with scarcely the appearance of a haling-path, the horses frequently sliding and staggering in the water, the haling-lines sweeping the gravel into the canal and the entanglement at the meeting of the boats incessant; while at the locks at each end of the short summit crowds of boatmen were always quarrelling, or offering premiums for a preference of passage, and the mine owners, injured by the delay, were loud in their just complaints.'[1]

It will be remembered that in 1790 the Birmingham company had eliminated the short summit level between Smethwick and Spon Lane on their main line by reducing it to the 473 ft Wolverhampton level, so Telford's reference to a short summit level requires further explanation. At Spon Lane, three locks led down to the original branch canal known as the Wednesbury old loop line which, since its 1786 extension to Walsall and district by the so-called Broadwaters Canal and branches, had been carrying a very heavy traffic. Because this Wednesbury line was at the Birmingham level, there was still a short summit with its attendant water supply difficulties so far as traffic between Birmingham and Wednesbury was concerned.

To eliminate this, Telford recommended a further reduction of this Smethwick/Spon Lane summit to the Birmingham level, the result being the great cutting which we see today. This was completed in 1829. It is 71 ft deep and is spanned at its deepest point by Galton bridge, a fine specimen of Telford's cast-iron bridgework with a span of 150 ft which was hailed as the largest canal bridge in the world. Below it ran a canal 40 ft wide with a broad towpath on each side. On this spacious scale the canal was later carried forward on a new direct line by means of lofty embankments to Tipton where it locked up to the Wolverhampton level. West of Tipton the old turtuous route via Wednesbury Oak was by-passed by a short cut-off from Bloomfield to Deepfields which included the 360-yard Coseley tunnel with a waterway width of 15 ft 9 in and two towing paths. The remainder of the main line between Deepfields, through Wolverhampton to Aldersley Junction was improved and deepened. This work on the main line was not completed until 1839, five years after Telford's death.

The Birmingham company had embarked on this great improvement scheme in anticipation of the completion of a new direct water route between the Midlands and the Mersey. This was the Birmingham & Liverpool Junction Canal, conceived by Telford and actively promoted by canal interests, headed by the Birmingham Company, as a counter to the rival railway scheme. The canal won the day, receiving its Act in May 1826. It was to be the last major victory for the old transport system over the new. It was also to be Telford's last major work and to build it he rallied to his aid the survivors of those engineers who had served him so well on the Ellesmere and Caledonian canals and on the Holyhead road: John Wilson and his two sons, Alexander Easton and William Provis.

The canal runs from Autherley Junction, on the Staffordshire & Worcestershire Canal near its junction with the Birmingham, to Nantwich where it joins the old Chester Canal close to its terminal basin. It was therefore enthusiastically welcomed by the proprietors of the Ellesmere & Chester canal, whose hitherto isolated waterways the new canal would now unite with the midland system. They also hoped that with the new company's influential support they might at last overcome the Trent & Mersey's opposition to their proposed branch to Middlewich. This hope was fulfilled. At long last this missing link was built from Barbridge on the old Chester canal to a junction with the Trent & Mersey at Wardle Lock, Middlewich, the ten miles of canal including a considerable masonry aqueduct over the river Weaver at Hoolgrave. It was completed in 1833.

The Birmingham & Liverpool Junction canal is carried over the Watling Street (A5) at Stretton by an iron trough aqueduct and there is also a short tunnel with towpath at Cowley (81 yds) near Gnosall. The latter was originally intended to be 690 yards long, but after a little over 200 yards had been driven the rock proved to be so rotten and treacherous that Telford decided to open out the workings and go through the greater part of the high ground in open cutting. Further to the north, a second iron trough aqueduct carries the canal over the Nantwich–Chester road. There are twenty-eight locks, falling to Nantwich, fifteen of which are concentrated in a flight at Audlem.

The lock houses and other buildings are distinguished by their low-pitched roofs with exceptionally wide eaves. Roofs of such low pitch were made possible at this period by the production in the Welsh quarries of slates of larger size and lighter weight, a circumstance with which Telford's work on the Holyhead Road had made him familiar.

The outstanding feature of the canal, however, is the magnitude of the earthworks which enable it to maintain a remarkably straight course through the rolling country of the Shropshire/Staffordshire border. No one can travel through this canal without being impressed by the contrast between it and the earlier contour canals engineered by Brindley and his school. It emphasizes the progress made in civil engineering during the canal era, illustrating that 'cut and fill' technique which would soon be used by the railway engineers and, in our own day, by the builders of motorways. It is significant that Telford's last canal is still the most direct route between the Black Country and the Mersey.

Nevertheless the earthworks caused Telford considerable trouble and anxiety as all works that are ahead of their time must do. Knowledge of soil mechanics was still rudimentary and, doubtless from a desire to economize in excavation, Telford chose far too steep an angle of slope for his cuttings. Repeated slips in Grub Street cutting, near Norbury, finally forced him to cut back the sides. The other notably deep cutting at Woodseaves, near Market Drayton, proved more stable though it has caused continual trouble with minor falls. Similarly, Telford experienced great difficulty in stabilizing his great embankments at Shelmore, Knighton, and Dorfold (Nantwich) and this was the more galling because Shelmore and Dorfold were undertaken as part of deviations made to placate local landowners at Norbury Park and Dorfold Hall. They did not appear on Telford's original plans.

The railway engineers had similar trouble with embankments owing in part to the use of clay and other unsuitable materials and also to the difficulty of compacting them. But whereas railway lines can always be lifted and packed if settlement occurs, a canal is not so accommodating. Shelmore Great Bank, as it was called, gave particular trouble; there were repeated slips and men were still struggling with it long after the rest of the canal was completed.[2] It was not until March 1835, six months after Telford's death, that a narrow channel, only a boat's width, over Shelmore enabled the first through passage to be made.

The completion of this canal not only provided a more direct and less heavily locked route between the industrial Midlands and the Mersey but also with Manchester via the new canal to Middlewich. Thirdly, a ten and a half mile branch canal from Norbury, through Newport to Wappenshall provided a link with another hitherto isolated canal system—the old Shrewsbury canal and the tub boat canals of industrial Shropshire. On this branch canal near Preston-upon-the-Weald-Moors is the Duke's Drive Aqueduct, an unusual and little known iron trough aqueduct with stone embellishments bearing the arms of the Duke of Sutherland.

The Birmingham & Liverpool Junction route threatened to take traffic away from the Trent & Mersey, but the days when that doyen of canal companies could play power politics with impunity were nearly over and while it certainly opposed the new route, its ineffective opposition seemed to lack the old fire and force. Perhaps its proprietors reflected that, compared with the rival railway scheme, the B. & L.J. was the lesser of two evils. At least it would bring its Manchester traffic to the Trent & Mersey between Middlewich and Preston Brook. It was this reasoning that had induced its proprietors to give belated consent to the junction at Middlewich.

Meanwhile the Trent & Mersey, like the Birmingham company, had been moved by the railway threat to put its own house in order and again it was Telford whose aid was sought. Here the equivalent of the Smethwick summit was Brindley's old tunnel at Harecastle. This was a bottleneck about which traders had been complaining bitterly but without avail for years. John Rennie had inspected the tunnel in 1820, reporting that the roof was only six feet above water level in places and so narrow that the brick lining had been worn to half its original thickness by the passage of boats. The mortar was so soft that bricks could be pulled out by hand. Yet four years passed before the company finally decided to act and Telford was called in. Having been delayed so long, the work of driving a new tunnel parallel with the old was pressed forward with all possible speed, Pritchard and Hoof being the contractors responsible. No less than fifteen shafts were sunk so that the work of driving the headings could be carried on simultaneously at thirty different points. In addition, cross headings were driven into the old tunnel so that boats could assist in the removal of spoil during the night. Such was the speed of operations that a seven foot diameter heading was completed in October 1825, and the tunnel was opened to traffic in March 1827. For sheer speed of execution, this was a feat of tunnelling that has seldom been surpassed, and when we recall that the old tunnel beside it had taken eleven years to build it is another striking example of the progress made in civil engineering technique.

Telford designed the new tunnel with a towing path after the model of his earlier tunnels at Chirk and Whitehouses but with slightly more generous dimensions. The presence of a towpath meant that it was a 'one way' tunnel, but Telford planned to enlarge the old tunnel similarly. This was never carried out, however, and southbound traffic continued to 'leg' through the old tunnel until the early years of this century when subsidence finally led to its closure.

From Hall Green at the north end of Harecastle Tunnels the Macclesfield canal runs northward along the western slopes of the Staffordshire and Derbyshire uplands for twenty-six miles to a junction with the Peak Forest canal at the top of the Marple locks. There is a single flight of twelve locks at Bosley which lifts the canal up to the 518 ft summit level of the Peak Forest. Construction was authorized in 1826 and the canal was opened in November 1831. It provided a shorter, though more heavily locked, route between the Potteries and Manchester and also brought water transport to the towns of Congleton and Macclesfield.

Thomas Telford prepared the original plans and estimates but had no hand in the actual construction for which William Crosley was responsible, Pritchard and Hoof being the main contractors. The monumental stonework of bridges and aqueducts on the Macclesfield suggests Rennie's work rather than Telford's, and Rennie's influence may indeed have been at work because Crosley had previously been resident engineer of the Lancaster canal, north end,[3] which, as we have seen, displays some of Rennie's finest work. There are a number of masonry aqueducts carrying the canal over the valleys of rivers and streams falling from the uplands into the Cheshire plain. The largest and finest of these is the Dane aqueduct at Bosley. Other examples are the aqueduct over the River Bollin at Langley, near Macclesfield, the Dean aqueduct at Bollington and the Red Acre aqueduct over the Poynton Brook at Michelford.

The Trent & Mersey company would not permit the sacred waters of their canal to be contaminated by this upstart newcomer. They insisted on building their own short branch to join the Macclesfield. This, curiously, leaves their main line on the south side, subsequently crossing over the latter as it descends the Cheshire locks, and continuing for over a mile to join the Macclesfield at Harding's Wood. Moreover, they ruled that the actual point of junction should be between two stop locks, one controlled by each company.

South-east of Birmingham the same pressures forced the Oxford canal company to make belated improvements, in this case the straightening of the northern half of their tortuous main line between Hawkesbury and Wolfamcote, just south of Braunston. This work was authorized in May 1829 and was completed in February 1834. It had the effect of shortening the line by nearly fourteen miles. Cuttings and embankments carry the new canal through ridges and across valleys which the old contour canal had taken many winding miles to avoid. A new tunnel, 250 yards long with towpaths on either side was driven at Newbold and three aqueducts carry the new canal over the Rugby–Lutterworth road and the rivers Swift and Avon north of Rugby. At Newbold the south entrance to the old tunnel at that place may still be seen adjacent to the churchyard and at right angles to the new tunnel, a circumstance which causes its chance discoverers some mystification. The old line was abandoned with the exception of the portions leading to Stretton, Brinklow, and Clifton Mill Wharves and that section forming the junction with the Grand Junction Canal at Braunston and providing access to the Braunston boatyard. Cast-iron roving bridges of most elegant design were erected wherever it was necessary to carry the new towpath over the old channel.

These Oxford canal improvements are frequently but erroneously attributed to Telford. In fact he had no hand in them. Several engineers were involved whose names we do not usually associate with canals. Sir Marc Brunel was first consulted, Charles Vignoles made the survey and William Cubitt acted as consultant while the work was in progress.

The improvement of the Oxford, however, was closely bound up with a canal scheme with which Telford was associated. This was for a London to Birmingham route which would avoid the heavy lockage on the Warwick line by keeping north of the Avon valley. It was this scheme which stirred the Oxford company to action, for it was first projected to run to Braunston and so would have cut the Oxford out of the through traffic altogether. When the Oxford company undertook to straighten their line, Anstey became the projected junction for the new route, but the canal was never built. In the light of history this was unfortunate for, despite the costly widening of the canal between Napton and Birmingham carried out by the new Grand Union company between 1931 and 1934, the heavy lockage on the Warwick line has remained a serious handicap to through traffic between Birmingham and London.

Those waterways associated with the Severn had long been impeded by the difficulties and hazards of navigating the tidal portion of that river below Gloucester. They enjoyed a very welcome fillip when the Gloucester & Berkeley Ship Canal was opened throughout in April 1827. This was not a belated reply to the railway threat, but an ambitious project of the mania period, authorized in 1793, which had been struggling towards completion ever since.

As planned in 1793 the canal would have been eighteen and a quarter miles long, 70 ft wide and 15 ft deep. But in 1818 the depth was increased to 18 ft and the length reduced to sixteen and three-quarter miles by the decision to join the Severn at Sharpness Point instead of at Berkeley Pill. Robert Mylne, the architect and builder of Blackfriars Bridge, was engineer of the canal until 1798. Finally, after a number of successors to Mylne had come and gone, Telford became responsible for completing the canal as engineer to the Exchequer Bill Loan Commissioners who authorized very substantial Government loans to enable the company to complete the canal.

Features of this canal are the fine ranges of warehouses at Sharpness and Gloucester; also the delightful little bridgemen's cottages with their pillared porches. The New docks and entrance lock at Sharpness were opened in November 1874, though the old entrance north of Sharpness Point was restored for emergency use during the last war.

To sum up, all these improvements, splendidly engineered though they were, came too late. Secure in their monopolies, the old canal companies, notably the Birmingham, the Trent & Mersey, and the Oxford, had put off essential development for too long. By so doing they had forfeited the sympathy of traders who were therefore only too ready to transfer their allegiance to the new railways. The sorry sequel is well known. Canal toll rates came tumbling down in the effort to meet the effect of railway competition, but all to no avail. The once proud canal companies were soon begging the railways to take them over in return for a guaranteed dividend. Some obtained powers to build railways themselves and used these powers as a bargaining counter. The Shropshire Union Railways and Canal Company, formed as a result of the amalgamation of the Ellesmere & Chester and the Birmingham & Liverpool Junction canals, was one such. It launched an ambitious programme of railway construction and had actually built one, the Shrewsbury & Stafford, before it was leased to the London and North-Western Railway in 1846.

With the coming of railways the canal system became virtually frozen. Railway companies were unlikely either to improve or to extend the systems of the canals they controlled, while such canal companies as remained independent became too impoverished to contemplate such developments. One example in the latter category was the Droitwich Junction canal, one and threequarter miles long with seven falling locks, which was promoted by the Worcester & Birmingham company in 1852 to link their canal at Hanbury Wharf with Brindley's old barge canal from the Severn to Droitwich. Another was the Slough Branch of the Grand Junction, completed in 1883.

With rare exceptions such as these, only the Birmingham canal network continued to develop and expand throughout the nineteenth century. For although the Birmingham Canal Navigations were leased by the London and North-Western Railway from 1846, the system continued to handle very heavy short-haul traffic from canal-side premises, much of which passed to the rail at special tranship-ment depots. Notable latterday improvements in the area were the Tame Valley Canal, eight and a half miles long, from the Walsall canal to a junction with the Birmingham & Fazeley at Salford, opened in 1844, and the Netherton tunnel which was built to relieve the restricted Dudley tunnel. Netherton is 3,027 yards long. It is 15 ft 9 in high and its width of 27 ft allows room for a towing path on each side. When opened in 1858 it was lit by gas, a contrast indeed to the dark little rat holes of the Brindley era and one which must have been most acceptable to the boatmen.

CHAPTER EIGHT

Forgotten Waterways

Not surprisingly, in the mania years of the early 1790s many over-optimistic canal schemes were promoted. Some of these never got beyond the preliminary survey stage and need not concern us. Some were completed, wholly or partially, but enjoyed such a brief working life that today they are almost forgotten, their courses only to be traced with difficulty. Thanks to recent research into canal records, most notably the work of Mr Charles Hadfield, we now know the background history of these shortlived projects, but only fieldwork can determine their actual routes and, in some cases, how much of that route was in fact constructed. For early writers and cartographers like Priestley are apt to describe as complete and to mark upon their maps canals which never existed except in the minds of their promoters. In such cases, only exploration can determine how much work was actually done.

Tracing and systematically recording these forgotten waterways upon the ground is a fascinating and worthwhile task for the industrial archaeologist who is not afraid of getting mud on his boots. For although they were unsuccessful, anything that called for such a prodigious expenditure of labour and skill is worth recording before it vanishes. Vanish they soon will under the obliterating blade of the bulldozer. For example, until a few years ago the line of the North Wilts canal on its course from the Wilts & Berks at Swindon to the Thames & Severn at Latton, near Cricklade was clearly visible from the bye road that runs beside it, but it is now being so rapidly filled in that soon it will be impossible to tell that such a canal ever existed. In this case, as in many others, however, the course of the North Wilts is clearly marked on earlier editions of the inch to the mile O.S. map. But to the course of other canals the O.S. map provides no such ready guidance.

Long-abandoned canals make a particularly pleasant subject for

fieldwork study because, almost invariably, they served predominantly rural areas. Most of them are to be found in southern England
in regions scarcely touched by nineteenth-century industrial
development. This was the main reason for their speedy eclipse.
Rural traffic proved too thin to nourish them and today we are
witnessing the disappearance of rural railway lines for the same
reason. Happily, as the bibliography at the end of this book reveals,
now, at the eleventh hour, some of these long-abandoned canals are
being made the subject of special studies.

Examples of abandoned canals in the East Midlands are the
thirty-three miles of the Grantham canal, winding through the
vale of Belvoir from the Trent at Nottingham to Grantham and,
further south, the River Wreak Navigation from its junction with
the River Soar (Leicester Navigation) at Cossington to Melton
Mowbray with its extension, the Oakham Canal, to Oakham. In 1904
de Salis reported that there was 'not much trade' on the Grantham
Canal and it was formally abandoned in 1936. Like other canals in
the area it had broad locks, eighteen in number, rising to Grantham.
The Wreak or Melton Mowbray Navigation, fifteen miles long with
twelve locks was abandoned in 1877 while its extension, the Oakham
Canal, had an even shorter life, having been abandoned in 1846.
There were nineteen broad locks in a distance of fifteen miles to
Oakham. This canal has recently been the subject of a special study
(see Bibliography).

In the West Midlands there are two abandoned canals of particular
interest running through beautiful country. These are the Kington
& Leominster and the Herefordshire & Gloucestershire canals. The
former was one of the more optimistic products of the mania period.
It was planned to ascend from the Severn at Stourport by a flight of
seventeen locks in three miles to a 207 ft summit level, thence passing through two tunnels, Pensax (3,850 yds) and Southnet (1,254
yds, earlier spelling Sousant or Sousnant) to join the northern side
of the Teme Valley whose slopes it followed through Tenbury to
Woofferton, crossing the rivers Rea and Teme by aqueducts. At
Woofferton it swung due south to Leominster where it turned west
once more to follow the Lugg valley to Kingsland, finally reaching
Kington, where it joined the Kington Tramway, by way of the
valley of the Arrow. There was a third tunnel at Putnal Field (330
yds) between Woofferton and Leominster. The route was surveyed

by Whitworth, and Thomas Dadford junior was the engineer.

Priestley[1] describes this canal as though it was complete, but it was speculative indeed to drive a canal involving such heavy works through this sparsely populated countryside, and in fact only the middle section from Broombank, immediately west of Southnet tunnel, to Leominster was ever completed. This was used to carry coal from the Mamble Pits to Leominster from 1794 until 1858 when the canal was acquired by the Shrewsbury & Hereford Railway, part of its bed being subsequently used by the Bewdley and Woofferton branch line, now itself abandoned. However, the wharf buildings at Broombank and Leominster still exist; so do Putnal Field tunnel, which gave its builders much trouble, and the fine masonry aqueduct over the Rea near Marlbrook which survives in remarkably good order. The centre span of the Teme aqueduct was deliberately destroyed during the last war.

Some mystery surrounds the two long tunnels. Southnet is said to have been completed, but although the eastern portal can be seen in the grounds of Southnet Farm, there is no trace of the western end. According to one local authority,[2] it would appear that construction of Pensax tunnel was begun, but was defeated by the nature of the ground. This story may apply to Southnet, for there is no evidence on the ground to show that any work was ever done on Pensax.

Until recently it was assumed that no work on the canal was done west of Leominster or east of Southnet, but recent field work[3] has disclosed traces of excavation and the pier bases of a second aqueduct over the Lugg near Kingsland; also some excavation in the grounds of Dumbleton Farm, east of Southnet.

'In 1797', writes Priestley, 'the entrance into the canal from the Severn [at Stourport] was opened', but this must have been wishful thinking for no trace of such an entrance can be found today. Had the canal been built as planned, water supply would have been something of a problem for it would have had no less than three summit levels in a length of forty-six miles, one on the line of the two long tunnels, a second between Wyson and Stockton Cross, and a third at Kington.

The Kington & Leominster canal has been dealt with at some length because it is an excellent example of the problems that can sometimes be posed by canal history which only field work can solve. No such mysteries surround the Herefordshire & Gloucestershire

Canal as it is known to have been completed throughout. Yet it is a parallel example of a canal with heavy and costly works promoted in the mania years through a rural area with no hope of earning a fair return on the capital expended. Running from the western branch of the Severn at Over, near Gloucester, by Newent and Ledbury to a terminus at Barr's Court basin, Hereford, such well-known names as Whitworth, Clowes and Henshall were associated with its construction. The canal was completed to Ledbury in 1798, but Hereford was not reached until 1845. Yet in 1881 the canal was closed when it was acquired by the Great Western Railway Company who then proceeded to build their Gloucester to Ledbury branch line over part of its bed. This railway by-passed a short section of canal between Newent and Dymock which includes the 2,192-yard Oxenhall tunnel. The north-western end of this tunnel is blocked by a landslide and according to the report of a recent canoe exploration, the interior is blocked by a roof fall.

There is a curious arched recess in the rock beside the south-eastern portal of Oxenhall the purpose of which is obscure. It would seem too large and elaborate to have been constructed to house the stop planks used to seal off the tunnel for underwater repairs and an alternative theory is that it was a donkey shelter, used while waiting for the boats to emerge.

Considerable portions of the eight and a half mile summit level of the canal from Ledbury to Monkhide remain including the tunnel at Ashperton (Walsopthorne). This last was to have been 1,192 yards long, but was reduced by open cutting to about 440 yards. As at Oxenhall, the north-western end has been closed by a landslide.* On the approach to Hereford the long embankment and aqueduct over the Lugg valley at Sutton Marsh survive, but, so far as is known, there is now no trace of the third tunnel, 440 yards long, under Aylstone Hill, Hereford.

In south-east England, the Thames & Medway canal was authorized in 1800, its object being to open a direct route for barge traffic between the two rivers, avoiding the long and difficult passage round the Hundred of Hoo. John Rennie acted as consultant and the

* A correspondent, Mr Frank Nelson, thinks this is no coincidence. He advances the theory that the more weather exposed and sunless north-western entrances may be more liable to subsidence. This would also account for the disappearance of the west end of Southnet Tunnel.

canal was completed in 1824, three years after his death. The one outstanding feature of this short canal from Gravesend to Rochester was the great tunnel through the chalk at Strood, by far the largest canal tunnel in this country. Its length, 3,909 yards, was only exceeded by Standedge but, unlike the latter, it was of great size; the crown of the arch was 27 ft above water level and its width of 26 ft 6 in included a 5 ft towpath. There was an 8 ft depth of water through the tunnel. As previously mentioned, the contractors were Pritchard and Hoof. The centre of the tunnel was later opened out to form a passing place for barges.

The canal was unsuccessful, but the size of the tunnel, large enough for a double line of railway, made it a valuable asset and it was eventually sold to the South-Eastern Railway to become part of their North Kent line. The rest of the canal was abandoned in 1934 and only the terminal basins then remained in use.

In 1763 Sir Richard Weston's old Wey Navigation was extended from Guildford to Godalming and in 1787 another ancient river navigation, that of the Sussex Arun, was extended to Newbridge, its tributary the Rother being made navigable to Midhurst in 1794. It was almost inevitable that with this extension of river navigation a canal link between the Wey and the Arun should be proposed to provide an inland water route between the Thames and the south coast and so, apart from its value for local trade, avoid the dangerous passage round the North Foreland. The Wey & Arun Junction canal was authorized in 1813 and opened in 1816, Josias Jessop having been responsible for the survey and for the design of the structural works. It was eighteen and a half miles long from the Wey at Stonebridge Wharf to the Arun at Newbridge. Moreover, the shortlived Portsmouth & Arundel canal opened in 1823, including a branch to Chichester, a cut across Thorney Island and the short Portsea Canal, provided an inland route between London and Portsmouth. With the exception of the Chichester Canal, the latter was abandoned in 1847, while the Wey & Arun canal, which had been badly engineered and consequently suffered from a chronic shortage of water on its short summit level, was abandoned in 1871. It would be superfluous to describe this forgotten water route in greater detail here because it has recently been the subject of an admirable study by Mr P. A. L. Vine (see Bibliography). Based on years of research and fieldwork and with a wealth of fascinating illustrations, this is a model of the kind of work which needs doing in this field.

The Basingstoke Canal, thirty-seven and a half miles long from the Wey Navigation at Woodham to Basingstoke Wharf, was authorized in 1778 and completed throughout in 1796. It had a chequered career. Evidently its proprietors soon realized that as a long branch serving a purely rural area the canal had no prosperous future, for optimistic proposals were made to extend its western end either to the Kennet & Avon at Newbury, to the Itchen Navigation, or to the Andover Canal at Andover. Needless to add, these came to nothing. Various attempts to revive the canal have been made and part of its length is still used for moorings. Five and a half miles of the canal at its western end were isolated by the collapse of the 1,200-yard tunnel at Greywell, near Odiham, in 1932, and this section is now dry and derelict.

The Andover Canal, twenty-two miles long from that town down the valleys of the Anton and Test to the tideway of Southampton Water at Redbridge was surveyed by Robert Whitworth, authorized in 1789 and completed in 1796. It is of limited interest to the field-worker because, following its closure in 1859, the greater part of its length was converted into a railway which became part of the London & South-Western Railway. Some sections of the canal survived, however, and may still be traced.

The Andover was connected with one of the most extraordinary projects of the canal mania, the Southampton & Salisbury Canal. This was to be built in two separate sections, Salisbury to Kimbridge and Redbridge to Southampton and Northam, the Andover Canal forming the link between them. The first section was apparently opened briefly for traffic as far as Alderbury Common, two miles from Salisbury.[4] The second section included a tunnel half a mile long under Southampton which caused considerable difficulty and was never completed or used. The digging of that part of the canal which ran parallel with Southampton Water provoked, understandably, some ribald criticism. Like the Andover canal, part of this portion was later used by the Andover–Southampton railway. At the time of writing the remains of this abortive project are being made the subject of field study. *

* The results have now been published in *The Bankrupt Canal*, Southampton and Salisbury, 1795–1808, by Edwin Welch. Pub. City of Southampton, 1966.

The region of Somerset and east Devon is a notable home of lost causes where canals are concerned. For here the dream of a canal to link the Bristol and English channels, and so avoid the passage round Land's End, was born in the Brindley era and lived on for seventy years before the railway age finally extinguished it. Schemes varied from Telford's grandiose ship canal on the scale of the Caledonian, which fortunately never left paper, to three more modest proposals for barge canals on different routes. These were the Dorset & Somerset Canal from the navigable Stour near Shillingston to a junction with the Kennet & Avon at Widbrook, near Bradford on Avon, authorized in 1796; the Chard Canal from Seaton through Axminster and Chard to the River Parrett; and finally the Grand Western Canal from the River Exe to the River Tone navigation at Taunton.

The proprietors of the Dorset & Somerset were obliged by their Act to construct first a branch from their intended main line at Frome through the Nettlebridge valley to tap the Somerset coalfield. Since the country this would traverse was very hilly and difficult, it was decided to make this branch a tub boat canal and to use a type of 'balance lock' (in fact a form of vertical lift) patented by James Fussell, who owned an ironworks at Mells. Part of this branch was built, for we know that Fussell's lift was demonstrated in 1800, but it was thought that all trace of it had disappeared until Mr Robin Atthill recently discovered no less than five lift pits, one of them undoubtedly the demonstration lift and the rest unfinished. Yet he describes in his book[5] how a local farmer's wife, who had lived most of her life beside this lost canal, stoutly denied that it had ever existed. Such are the difficulties—and the rewards—of fieldwork.

These remains of the Nettlebridge Branch on Mendip, including ivy-covered aqueducts at Coleford, and Murtry, represent the only portion of the Dorset & Somerset ever constructed. The area is a fruitful one for exploration, for up the neighbouring valleys of the Wellow and Cam brooks ran the two branches of the Somerset Coal canal. These united, like the brooks, at Midford, the 'main line' running thence to a junction with the Kennet & Avon immediately west of the Dundas aqueduct. The two branches terminated at Radstock and Timsbury where plateways ran to the various collieries. At the time the canal was authorized in 1794, the Somerset coalfield was extremely active and expanding. Both the Kennet & Avon and the Wilts & Berks companies welcomed the project, foreseeing a profitable trade in Somerset coal developing. The difference of level to be surmounted was so steep, however, and the valleys so deep and narrow that canal construction was peculiarly difficult and costly. Indeed the Radstock line was never completed as a canal, a descending tramway apparently being substituted between Wellow and Midford. According to Priestley,[6] a tramway was substituted throughout after twenty years, although the line of the original canal can still be traced between Radstock and Wellow.

On the Timsbury Branch the canal had to climb 130 ft in little more than one and a quarter miles between Midford and Combe Hay. Here Robert Weldon's 'caisson lock', one of the most fearsome and extraordinary forms of canal lift ever devised (see chapter nine) was at first tried. It was unsuccessful and all trace of it has disappeared although its memory is perpetuated in the name of Caisson House near by. An inclined plane, the line of which can still be traced, was then substituted, the coal being transhipped in boxes between the boats and waggons on the plane. Not surprisingly, this proved so uneconomical that in 1802 it was decided to build a flight of twenty-seven narrow locks. To supply these locks with water, two pumping engines had to be provided at Dunkerton and Combe Hay. The date when the latter ceased work is not known, but the Dunkerton engine stopped pumping in November 1898[7] owing to lack of traffic and the canal thereafter fell derelict. The sharply curving flight of locks with their unusually deep chambers may still be seen.

As authorized in 1811, the Bridgewater & Taunton canal was to have run from the Bristol Avon at Morgan's Pill, down through east Somerset, crossing the rivers Yeo, Axe, Brue, Carey and Tone to a terminal basin at Fire Pool Mills, Taunton. Not surprisingly, in 1824 the company obtained powers to abandon this scheme in favour of the more modest one for a canal from the river Parret at Bridgewater to Taunton. Although this canal survives as a water channel, it is no longer navigable, chiefly owing to the construction of fixed bridges across it during the last war. It is mentioned here because its completion in 1827 materially affected both the Chard and Grand Western canal schemes, both now electing to join this new canal instead of the Tone Navigation as originally planned.

As a coast to coast waterway, the Chard canal, like the Dorset & Somerset, remained a dream, but it was revived in 1834 as a purely local project to link Chard with the Bridgewater & Taunton at Creech St Michael. It was completed in May 1842 with four inclined planes at Thornfalcon, Wrantage, Ilminster, and Chard Common and two tunnels at Lillesdon and Crimson Hill, the latter 1,800 yards in length.[8] A locally promoted railway between Taunton and Chard was incorporated in 1861, but two years later its powers were taken over by the Bristol & Exeter Company who built the line and opened it in September 1866.[9] To what extent this railway made use of the line of the canal and whether any traces of the latter remain is not known. The canal was bought by the Bristol and Exeter Railway in 1867 and closed.[10]

The Grand Western canal scarcely lived up to its grandiose title. Incorporated in 1796, nothing was done until 1810 when, as in the case of the Dorset & Somerset, cutting began on the summit level at Loudwell with the object of completing first the proposed branch from that summit to Tiverton, seven and three-quarter miles from its junction with the main line near Ayshford. This was in anticipation of considerable traffic in stone and lime from quarries in the vicinity of Burlescombe, and the work was completed in 1814. There matters rested until 1827 when the opening of the Bridgewater & Taunton gave the Grand Western proprietors a fresh incentive to extend their canal to Taunton. To do this, however, meant overcoming a difference in level of 265 ft, and they had so far forgotten the dream of a barge canal from coast to coast that they decided to achieve this limited objective by building a tub boat canal using lifts instead of locks. This was on the advice of James Green the engineer of the Bude Canal in Cornwall.

As opened in 1838, there were eight vertical lifts and one inclined plane on this section of the canal, the former being not dissimilar from that built by Fussell on the Dorset & Somerset.

In 1863 the Grand Western was bought by the Bristol & Exeter Railway and in the following year powers were obtained to abandon the canal between Firepool Bridge, Taunton and the summit at Loudwell.[11] There is now no trace of it in Taunton, but considerable remains exist elsewhere which merit investigation. The summit section to Tiverton continued to be used for stone traffic from Whipcott and Burlescombe wharves, but on a diminishing scale. In 1904 de Salis[12] reported that only two boats were still at work on the canal. These worked chained together, and from his description of them they were evidently survivors of the tub boats used on the Taunton–Loudwell section. Traffic ceased entirely after the First World War although some miles of the canal from the Loudwell end are still in water. So perished the dream of a canal from the Bristol to the English channels.

Finally, mention must be made of the canals of West Devon and Cornwall. These were purely local projects promoted either by mining interests or to transport sea sand for use on the land as a substitute for lime. For a full account of them the reader is referred to Mr Charles Hadfield's *Canals of Southern England*. Here, mention need only be made of the Bude Canal, the most extensive and remarkable waterway in this group.

Today the Bude canal consists simply of a sea lock at Bude with a stretch of broad canal extending inland from it for two miles to Helebridge. Prior to 1891, however, Helebridge was the starting point of a tub boat canal which, with its branches, extended for nearly forty miles. Had the original plans materialized it would have crossed Cornwall to join the Tamar, but even as built it was the most extensive canal of its kind in Britain. The main line extended through Red Post and North Tamerton to Druxton, three miles north of Launceston. There was a branch from Red Post to Brendon, Holsworthy and Blagdonmoor, while a feeder branch ran from Brendon to a reservoir at Alfardisworthy.[13] This reservoir, now known as Tamar Lake, and nine miles of the feeder are now used for water supply purposes.

The system was worked entirely by inclined plane lifts, six in all. Two of these, at Marhamchurch (Helebridge) and Hobbacott Down lifted the main line 345 ft above its level at Helebridge, while three further planes lowered the canal to its terminus at Druxton. The sixth plane was on the Blagdonmoor Branch near Brendon and raised boats to the summit level of the canal near the junction of the feeder from Alfardisworthy. The Hobbacott Down lift was powered by a bucket descending in a well, but all the others by water wheels. All were engineered by James Green. In addition to these lifts, the works included an aqueduct over the Tamar near Burmsdon and a tunnel of 'considerable length'[14] near Holsworthy. Yet so far as is known the remains of this most remarkable canal have never been systematically investigated or recorded.

17 Smethwick Cutting and Galton Bridge, Birmingham Canal

TELFORD'S LAST CANALS

18 Shelmore 'Great Bank', Birmingham and Liverpool Junction Canal

19 The little-known Duke's Drive aqueduct on the Newport Branch

'SHROPSHIRE UNION'

20 Lock Cottage, Eyton-upon-the-Wealdmoors

21 Putnal Field Tunnel

FORGOTTEN WATERWAY: THE KINGSTON AND LEOMINSTER CANAL

22 Bed of the Canal and Lock Cottage near Leominster

23 Inclined lift of bucket-in-well type with fly governor

TWO ILLUSTRATIONS FROM FULTON'S *Treatise on Canal Navigation*, 1796

24 Vertical lift with caissons confined to upper level and boats freely suspended. Fly governor and lift actuated pumps to return caisson water

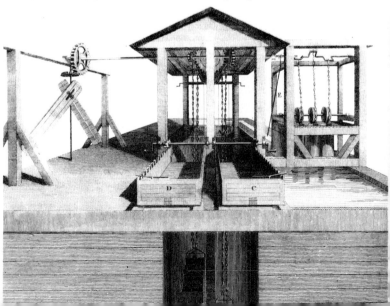

25 A caisson at the bottom of the lift

INCLINED PLANE LIFT AT FOXTON, GRAND UNION CANAL

26 The lift under construction

27 A Wherry at New Mills, Norwich, early morning. An illustration from Emerson's *English Lagoons*, 1893

WATERWAY CRAFT

28 A pair of 'Number One' narrow boats at the height of their glory

29 and 30 Two illustrations showing a narrow boat cabin interior from *Rob Rat*, 1878. Note the entire absence of decoration

31 An illustration from Robertson's *Life on the Upper Thames*, 1875. Perhaps the earliest representation of canal boat decoration

32 The steamer *Vulcan* under way on the Grand Junction Canal

STEAM POWER ON THE CANAL

33 Engine of Leeds and Liverpool Canal
Steamer

34 Engine of Fellows, Mor[...]
and Clayton steamer *Vicer[...]*

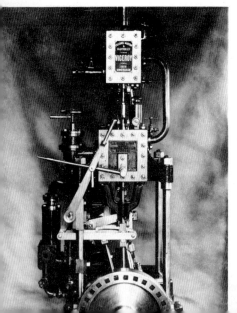

CHAPTER NINE

Water Supply and Conservation

For the engineers of the canals water supply was of paramount importance because it was this factor alone which determined the tonnage of traffic which a canal could pass. This may seem to be a truism, yet it is frequently overlooked by those who advocate making greater use of our canal system for commercial transport. Their argument is usually based on the undoubted fact that it requires less power to move a ton of goods by water than by either road or rail. They ignore the cost of providing the water, the essential 'track'. This blind spot may be due to the fact that our canal system has been but lightly used for so many years that we have forgotten the elaborate and often costly water supply provisions that were made in their hey-day and which alone enabled them to carry the tonnage they did before the railway era.

In some cases, as on the Ellesmere Canal at Llantisilio, engineers were able to tap the upper reaches of rivers for a supply to their summit levels. This was a cheap and usually reliable form of supply, but even here the amount of water so extracted was often restricted by statute, or the canal company were placed under obligation to return the water to the river at a lower level. The most usual method of supply, as we have seen, was to construct catchment reservoirs on suitable sites, connecting them to the summit level by feeder channels, sometimes in the form of navigable branch canals as at Wendover on the Grand Junction or at Welford on the old Grand Union.

In some cases where the supply reservoir was built at a level considerably above that of the canal, it was necessary to construct a stepped weir at the point where the feeder joins the canal in order to break the fall of the water. A good example of such a weir is to be seen at the east end of Butterley Tunnel on the Cromford Canal, conveying the supply from Butterley reservoir.

Sometimes streams flowing across the line of the canal were intercepted and used as direct feeders, but this practice is objectionable. Even the smallest stream deposits a surprising volume of silt in the canal and so greatly increases the need for dredging. For the same reason, silt rapidly accumulates in catchment reservoirs and the capacity of most of our canal reservoirs has been considerably reduced by lack of dredging.

Often it became necessary to construct additional reservoirs to supply the needs of the traffic. Thus trade on the Trent & Mersey was so heavy that Brindley's original underground supply from the Goldenhill colliery soon became quite inadequate. It had to be supplemented by reservoirs constructed first at Rudyard, feeding via the Leek and Caldon branches, and later at Knipersley. As a pioneer, Brindley may be forgiven a failure to estimate correctly the needs of future traffic, but in the case of some of his successors the fault is less excusable. Despite his other merits, as a canal engineer, John Rennie was especially weak in the matter of water supplies. Had traffic developed on the scale that their promoters envisaged, the water supply to the Rochdale and Kennet & Avon canals would have proved quite inadequate. Moreover, both these canals exhibit the cardinal error of a very short summit level.

To ensure against rapid fluctuations of level due to temporary excess of demand over supply, most canal engineers from Brindley onwards provided a long summit level or, where this was not possible, increased its depth. For example, on the Leeds & Liverpool, Robert Whitworth not only by resurveying increased the length of the summit pound from one to six miles, but he gave it an extra depth of two feet. Of the more celebrated canal engineers, William Jessop was probably the most generous in the provision of water supplies.

On the busiest canals, water drawn from reservoirs had to be supplemented by pumping engines, either to pump back the lockage water or to provide additional supplies. Where a canal had a busy branch falling from its main line at an intermediate level it frequently became necessary to install a pumping engine to return the branch lockage water to the main line. The old Wednesbury branch of the Birmingham Canal was a case in point. At one time, in addition to six reservoirs, no less than seventeen pumping engines were required to meet the needs of the traffic on the Birmingham Canal Navigations. Sometimes, as at Braunston on the Grand Junction special storage reservoirs were provided to hold the water used in lockage prior to its return to the summit by pump. In the case of a long summit, such reservoirs might be provided to store excess summit water in rainy seasons instead of letting it run to waste over spill weirs or through flood paddles. An example of this is Tardebigge reservoir, near the top of the famous flight of thirty locks on the Worcester & Birmingham Canal, although the pumps used to return the water to the summit level no longer exist.

The Thames & Severn and the Kennet & Avon are examples of canals which depended entirely on pumped water supplies. In the former case, this was drawn from springs at Thames Head where the site of the pumping engine can still be traced. On the Kennet & Avon, as we have seen, the original pumping plants still exist on site although they no longer operate. Another example of an early canal pumping plant to survive on site is the Lea Wood Pumping Station on the Cromford Canal, but in most cases the engines have gone though the buildings may remain.

The oldest canal pumping engines still in existence are the New-comen type engine formerly at Hawkesbury Junction on the Coventry Canal[1] and the Birmingham Canal's Ocker Hill engine, an early Boulton & Watt, now in the Birmingham Museum of Science & Industry and shortly to be re-erected there. On the demolition of the Hawkesbury engine house by British Waterways, the former engine was acquired by the Newcomen Society and re-erected in 1963 at Dartmouth,, the inventor's birthplace, as a permanent memorial to Thomas Newcomen.

Nowadays, those who travel the canals for pleasure are apt to regard the stop locks provided at the junction of one canal with another as archaic survivals of bygone intercompany rivalries, but they had a very practical significance in the days of dense traffic. Then, no company could afford to make another a present of its precious water supplies no matter how friendly their relations might be.

It was equally vital to prevent loss of water through leakage, and for this puddled clay was the infallible specific. In the clay lands of the Midlands a comparatively thin layer of puddle would suffice, but in the chalk, and particularly on the oolite, it was quite otherwise. A section through the Thames & Severn canal near Cirencester, made in the course of recent highway improvements revealed a

K

lining of puddle not less than 30 inches thick[2] laid on a course of rubble stone. Even this was not always sufficient to prevent leakage, although this was not necessarily the fault of the puddle. In periods of high rainfall, the flow of water through fissures and faults in the strata generates sufficient pressure to blow up the puddle in the bed of the canal. When conditions return to normal, the pressure drops and the water in the canal flows away through the blow holes. The section of the Thames & Severn Canal east of Sapperton Tunnel and the Kennet & Avon Canal in the Avon Valley suffered particularly from this trouble and it was never satisfactorily overcome. At Sapperton it defied even such an eminent civil engineer as Sir Benjamin Baker and finally the Gloucestershire County Council resorted to the desperate expedient of lining the whole bed with concrete. On the Kennet & Avon the pound worst affected has been dewatered. The section of the Lancaster Canal between Tewitfield locks and the Stainton feeder is similarly troubled, particularly in the vicinity of Turnpike bridge at Holme.

To avoid waste of water in lockage, the summit locks should not be substantially deeper than those below, otherwise the water released from them will tend to run to waste over the weirs. The converse is also true as may be seen at Weir lock where the Oxford Canal leaves the River Cherwell near Thrupp. This lock has a very small fall, so in order to take enough water in from the river to supply the deeper locks lower down the canal, its chamber has been broadened to a diamond shape.

In the case of a long level pound where the flow of water is always in the same direction, drawing water through the locks at the downstream end may cause a considerable reduction in the water level at that end. In other words the flow of water through such a long level is so slow, particularly if the pound is obstructed by weeds, that at the upstream end the pound may be full and the water running to waste over the spill weirs while at the downstream end it may be as much as six inches or more 'below weir'. We are extraordinarily ignorant about the surveying methods used by the canal engineers, and we do not know whether, in taking the levels for such a long pound they allowed any fall in the bed of the canal. The gradient will vary according to the cross section of the canal and the amount of water passing, but readings taken recently on the fourteen mile pound of the Ellesmere canal between the Llantisilio intake from the Dee and the locks at New Marton show that with a flow of eight million gallons per day the gradient is 0·88 in per mile, or the equivalent of a drop of 12 inches in the length of the pound.[3]

On a long pound, serious flooding would ensue in the event of the canal bursting its banks on an embankment and on later canals, where embankments were common, it became usual to narrow the canal between masonry walls at the embankment approaches and there to install a special 'stop.gate' so that the embankment could be sealed off in an emergency. Alternatively, the simpler 'stop planks' are used for this purpose, these planks being slid successively into 'stop grooves' formed in the retaining walls. These grooves are also provided above and below each lock so that the lock can be 'stopped off' for repairs.

On canals, where water was precious, it was essential that leakage of water through the lock gates was minimal, and lock maintenance, especially the making and fitting of new lock gates or the fitting of a new elm sill is a highly skilled job. The heavy oak gates must be true and 'out of wind' if they are to fit snugly against the sill and also into the hollow quoin in the lock wall in which the gate swings. It used to be said of a good lock gate maker that when he had fitted a new top gate and the water had been let in against it he could sit and eat his lunch on the masonry sill inside the lock and not get his bottom wet.

The need to economize water in lockage produced the device of the side pond on the Grand Junction and other heavily used canals. This consists of a masonry chamber beside the lock at an intermediate level, the two being interconnected by a ground paddle. By this means half a full lock of water can be discharged into the side pond before its paddle is closed and the remainder released into the pound below. The water thus stored in the side pond may then be re-used partially to fill the empty lock. In theory, half a lock of water could be saved at each lockage by the use of side ponds, and as the average wide lock on the Grand Junction passes 56,000 gallons of water each time a boat goes through, this amounts to a substantial saving. In practice, however, the saving was not so great, for if the side pond is used conscientiously to maximum effect the time taken to lock through is greatly increased. Consequently boatmen, to whom time was money, either neglected to use the side ponds altogether or, at best, made only a token use of the side pond paddle. Supervision of every lock by the canal company was obviously out of the question and stern notices threatening dire penalties for failure to use the side ponds had no effect. Most of the boatmen could not read them anyway.

On certain busy narrow canals, duplicate narrow locks were provided beside the originals and connected by paddles so that one acted as a side pond to the other. The Cheshire Locks by which the Trent & Mersey canal descends from Harecastle summit towards Middlewich were duplicated in this way and so were the three locks at Hillmorton on the reconstructed northern section of the Oxford canal.

Most extravagant of all in the use of water is the lock staircase. In theory, if all the 'steps' in the staircase are equal, a descending boat carries with it only one lock-full, as in an ordinary flight. But a boat ascending a five lock staircase such as Bingley five-rise must needs draw five locks of water away from the summit. This inordinate consumption may be reduced by the use of side ponds as at Foxton and Watford on the old Grand Union, but at Bingley there are no side ponds. This led Priestley, writing in 1831, to describe Bingley five-rise as an 'unfortunate arrangement' which 'must always cause a great waste of water, till remedied by dividing the fall'.[4]

The great expense, both in water and time, of long flights of locks, and particularly of lock staircases, stimulated canal engineers to evolve different forms of boat lift, some vertical and others inclined, for use where the change of level to be overcome was particularly great. Unfortunately, although these embodied clever ideas, some of them later applied with success elsewhere,[5] the ingenuity of their inventors generally made too exacting demands upon the technological competence of the time in translating their ideas into 'hardware'. Consequently, although some of them worked well when first installed, in constant use the lifts were dogged either by the breaking of chains or ropes or by fractures and failures of the somewhat complex mechanism employed to operate them.

According to William Chapman,[6] Edmund Leach claimed to have invented the inclined plane canal lift in 1774. In that year Leach proposed for the Bude Canal a series of inclines in which small boats would be floated into two tanks or caissons moving over rollers on the inclined plane and interconnected by a rope or chain passing over a drum at the top of the plane. Since a boat displaces its own weight of water, the weight of the two caissons would always remain the same no matter whether the boats they held were empty or loaded. Consequently, Leach argued that the plane could always be made self-acting by adding more water to the descending caisson. The bottom of such a plane presents no difficulty; in this case the caissons submerged in the lower pound, allowing the boats to float out. At the top of the plane, however, the boats had to cross a 'sill', or 'bridge', as it was sometimes called, before descending a short reverse plane into the upper pound of the canal. Leach proposed to overcome this problem by fitting rollers in the bottom of his caisson so that, when it had been drawn upon the sill and the water from it discharged into the upper pound, the boat could readily be launched from it. This plan of Leach's was never carried out.

Unknown to Leach, at the time he propounded his plan, Davis Ducart* was constructing three inclined plane lifts on the Coalisland Canal in Co. Tyrone. On the first of these Ducart used rollers, but not caissons, the small tub boats being drawn directly over them. It was thus little more than the ancient Pont aux Rouleaux except that it was a double plane, the ascending and descending craft being interconnected by rope so that loaded boats drew up the empties. In the next two inclines at Coalisland, however, Ducart introduced four-wheeled cradles running on rails onto which the boats could be floated at the bottom of the planes. These inclines, too, were self-acting except that horse gins were used to work the cradles over the sills at the top of the planes. Ducart died about 1778 and for lack of funds his canal was never completed, only a few boats being passed over the planes 'by way of trial'.[7]

The ironmasters William and Richard Reynolds were responsible for the design and construction in 1788 of the first canal inclined plane to work in England. This was on a short private canal which was built to convey coal and ironstone from Oakengates to their ironworks at Ketley. The plane was used to overcome a vertical fall of 73 ft to the ironworks, so the gradient was with the load and the plane was self-acting. Wheeled cradles running on iron plateways were used to carry the tub boats, the wheels being of unequal diameters so

---

* Ducart is a somewhat mysterious figure. He is described by Chapman as 'an Engineer in the Sardinian Service who settled in Ireland' and his name is variously spelt by contemporaries. According to Tew it was properly Daviso De Arcort.

as to maintain the cradles in a horizontal position on the plane. Instead of a sill at the top of the plane, there were two parallel lock chambers, the bottoms of which were inclined so that they formed the top part of the plane. When water was admitted to the lock, the ascending boat floated off its cradle. Conversely, when the lock was drawn off, a descending craft settled on to its submerged cradle. *

Since economy in the use of water was the object of the exercise, one would expect to learn that the two lock chambers were interconnected in the manner described earlier in this chapter. Curiously enough, this does not appear to have been the case, for we are told[8] that water from the locks was discharged into a reservoir from which, in dry seasons, it was pumped back to the summit by a steam engine.

At the same time, William Reynolds built another short tub-boat canal to convey coal and ironstone from Wombridge to the ironworks at Donnington Wood, on the same level. These two canals, however, did not originate the tub boat canal system in Shropshire. The parent of the system was the Donnington Wood Canal with which the latter connected. This ran for five and a half miles from underground levels at Donnington Wood colliery to a coal wharf at Pave Lane on the Newport–Wolverhampton road. Tub boats loading 3 tons were used on it. The canal was projected in 1764 and completed in 1768 by Earl Gower and Company, a partnership consisting of Lord Gower and the brothers John and Thomas Gilbert. Since the former was the 'Canal Duke's' brother-in-law and John Gilbert his agent, there was thus a close connection between this little canal and the pioneer Bridgewater, indeed the methods used at Donnington Wood and on the underground canals at Worsley paralleled each other so closely that it is impossible to say which was the precursor.

Thus between the main line of the Donnington Wood canal at Hugh's Bridge and the branch canal to Lilleshall limestone quarries 42 ft 8 in below, coal and limestone were interchanged by containers raised and lowered by counterbalanced hoists through twin vertical shafts.[9] The same system was used between the underground levels at Worsley until it was superseded by an inclined plane of the Reynolds type. A similar plane may have been introduced at Donnington Wood colliery at the same time.[10]

* This is the generally accepted, but conjectural, mode of working. But Chapman states that the laden boat 'was floated on its carriage' into the full lock.

Following the success of Reynolds' Ketley Canal, the Shropshire Canal was promoted in 1788 by a consortium of local ironmasters expressly to serve their joint interests. Running for seven and a half miles from the Donnington Wood canal to the Severn at Coalport, there were three considerable inclined planes, the first at Wrockwardine Wood, 320 yards long, lifting boats 120 ft from the Donnington Wood level to the summit, the second at Windmill Hill descending 126 ft in 600 yards, and the third descending 207 ft in 350 yards at the Hay. From the foot of the Hay plane the canal ran parallel with the Severn to wharves at Coalport where goods were transhipped from the tub boats into river barges.

Curiously enough, although William Reynolds was primarily responsible for laying out the Shropshire Canal and although his system of carrying the boats in wheeled cradles on the planes was adopted, his device of twin locks at the top of the plane was not. This meant that the cradles had to surmount a sill. The cradles carried an extra pair of larger diameter wheels mounted inboard at their uphill end which connected with two rails on the short reverse plane leading into the upper pound of the canal. This prevented the cradle assuming too steep an angle as it overtopped the sill. Steam engines* were used to haul the cradles over the sills and, by means of dog clutches and gearing, could also supply additional power for haulage on the main planes. On the first incline at Wrockwardine Wood the steam power required was considerable as the load was generally against the gradient.

The last incline of this Shropshire series to be built was that at Trench, completed about 1795, to connect the Shropshire tub boat system, via the Wombridge canal, with the Shrewsbury Canal. It was built by the latter company who also purchased the Wombridge canal. It worked on the same principle and was by far the longest lived of any canal incline in Britain, going out of use in 1921. The locks on the Shrewsbury Canal were built with chambers 81 ft long to pass four tub boats at a time. At their lower end they were unique in having guillotine gates counterbalanced by a chain and weight sinking in a pit. According to contemporary accounts,[11] they once

---

* These were of the Heslop type, a primitive form of compound in which a closed 'high-pressure' cylinder exhausted into a second cylinder of open-topped Newcomen type. It was one of a number of engines designed at this time to circumvent the Watt Patent monopoly.

had intermediate guillotine gates so that they could pass two tub boats without waste of water, but the present chambers reveal no trace of such a provision. After the opening of the Newport and Wappenshall branch of the Birmingham & Liverpool Junction canal, an increasing proportion of the waterborne traffic from the Shropshire industrial district passed directly to that canal via a tramway and the Humber Arm rather than by the Trench inclined plane. Only one and a quarter miles of the Shropshire Canal from Tweedale to Blissers Hill Furnaces survived into the twentieth century. On this level lengthy trains of tub boats conveyed coal and iron ore to the furnaces. This was loaded in containers, four to a boat.[12]

In Cornwall, Lord Stanhope continued to mull over the idea of the Bude Canal, using inclined planes, but in 1793 he was advocating gradual inclines up which boats could be hauled directly by horses on cradles having wheels six feet in diameter.[13] Alternatively, he proposed a curious variant of Leach's original plan for roller planes; in this the rollers would successively move forward under the ascending boat, returning by means of chains attached to their pivots and passing over pulleys to counterweights, when the boat left them. Stanhope argued that friction would thereby be reduced and the bottom of the boat would be better supported.

According to the introduction to his book,[14] it was Robert Fulton who, in correspondence with Stanhope on the subject of steam navigation, persuaded him to drop these ideas in favour of his own, as subsequently described and illustrated in the above mentioned book. He advocated both single and double planes as traffic required, using tub boats with small wheels recessed into the hull running in trough rails up the planes. To haul these boats over the upper sills and to provide power on the main planes, Fulton proposed a waterwheel or, in cases where the lift required was great, an iron bucket. The latter was filled with water from the upper pound and descended a vertical shaft. On reaching the foot of this shaft, a trip valve in the bottom of the bucket opened, discharging its contents through a culvert into the lower pound of the canal. The empty bucket was then drawn back to the surface by a counterweight. To regulate the speed of winding, Fulton shows what he calls 'a pair of centrifugal fans'. This was simply a monstrously enlarged version of the device used to regulate the speed of the striking train in clocks. In his drawings, Fulton places this fearsome mechanism in a position best calculated to knock an unwary boatman insensible and send him spinning in to the upper pound of the canal. Another defect of Fulton's arrangement is plainly apparent in his illustrations. The wheels of his boats were of equal diameter and they therefore assumed the same angle as the plane so that, if the plane was steep, the cargo would tend to spill.

As we saw in the last chapter, all the inclined planes on the Bude canal were actually built by James Green and reputedly designed by him, that at Hobbacott Down being powered on the bucket principle and the rest by waterwheel. It would appear that they conformed closely to those described and illustrated in Fulton's book, though there is much doubt as to whether James Green's work inspired the book or vice versa. Certainly Fulton claimed the ideas as his own although he never applied them himself whereas James Green went on to build other inclined planes elsewhere. He was responsible for the incline at Weare Giffard on the Rolle canal near Torrington (waterwheel); for the Wellesford incline on the Grand Western canal (bucket-in-shaft); for the incline on the short Morris's canal at Llandore (water-turbine) and the inclines on the Chard and Gwendraeth Valley (Kidwelly & Llanelly) canals. On the last named, the power is described as 'hydraulic pumps',[15] but since the gradient here would be with the load this may refer to the application of another idea of Fulton's. This was to utilize the power of a descending boat and to regulate its speed by means of pumps which returned water to the upper pound and which were driven by a crankshaft direct coupled to the winding drum. For the two inclines on the Chard canal, Green abandoned Fulton's scheme of wheeled boats. At Chard Common he carried the boats in wheeled cradles as on the Shropshire tub boats canal, but using only a single line of rails. At Ilminster, however, the boats were floated into six-wheeled caissons running on a double line of railway.[16] There is some doubt whether the other two lifts on the Chard canal at Thornfalcon and Wrantage were of vertical or inclined plane type, but since the difference in level was only 28 ft and 31 ft respectively as compared with 78 ft at Chard Common and 94 ft at Ilminster, the probability is that they were vertical.

Green underpowered his bucket-operated lifts at Hobbacott Down and Wellesford by making his buckets too small and in both cases they had to be supplemented by steam power. He appears to have

supervised the working of the Bude Canal for a time, for in a confi-
dential report * on the working of the canal which Alexander Easton
wrote to Telford in September 1824,[17] he states that Green was a
'strenuous advocate' of a certain Mr Blackmore's refusal to pay his
tolls on the canal and hints darkly: 'there must be pecuniary obliga-
tions or motives in this to sway Mr Green'. Though the foremost
canal engineer in the west of England, Green was dismissed as
engineer to the Grand Western and the Gwendraeth Valley canals
almost simultaneously in 1836,[18] but whether this was due to the
moral peccadillos of the engineer or to the practical defects of his lift
machinery, which were many, will probably never be determined.

Easton, in the above mentioned report, gives Telford some information on the working of Green's planes on the Bude canal.

> Trade? [he writes] Demand is not regular but brisk and slack at
> intervals as the farmers find employment on their farms, so that
> nothing less than 12 months is sufficient to form an idea of the
> probable trade. Some days 50 boats will pass up the planes, but on
> an average it does not exceed more than 35. I could not calculate
> on the engine rising more than 60 boats each working day. Not
> having seen both Buckets† in a working state, I cannot with
> confidence state the number of boats that might be raised by them
> each day. The observation I have made from one Bucket working
> I am inclined to think that 100 Boats might be raised = 400T,
> at 5 working days = 2000T per week at 1/9d per ton will be £175
> per week or £8,400 per year.

Mention should be made at this point of two latter-day inclined
planes, both using 'wet' caissons moving on wheels and rails and both
designed to carry, not tub boats but full sized canal craft. The first
was built in 1849–50 at Blackhill on the Monkland Canal to supplement a flight of locks which had to be closed for lack of water during
the summer of 1849, bringing the heavy coal traffic to a standstill.
The lift was designed by James Leslie, Messrs Yule and Wilkie being
the contractors for the machinery. The caissons were built to carry a

---

* The company had applied for a loan from the Exchequer Bill Loan
Commissioners for whom Telford acted as consulting engineer.
† The planes were not counterbalancing, although double. This was the
method advocated by Fulton where, as in this case, the load was against the
gradient.

barge 70 ft long by 13 ft 4 in beam and the incline was self-acting but supplemented by steam power, which could be used to raise one caisson independently if necessary. The lift was used to supplement the locks when water was scarce during the summer months and worked well until 1887, by which time the pits in the vicinity had been worked out and a declining coal trade no longer justified its maintenance.[19]

The last inclined plane lift to work in this country was that at Foxton on the line of the old Grand Union canal. It consisted of two counterbalanced caissons each capable of floating a pair of narrow boats or one wide boat and was designed by Gordon Thomas, the then Chief Engineer of the Grand Junction Company and his brother, James Thomas, after practical experiments at Bulbourne. It was built by J. and H. Gwynne and Co. of Hammersmith and opened for traffic in July 1900. Each caisson ran sideways down the concrete apron of the plane on eight sets of wheels and rails, steam power being used to overcome friction. The vertical fall was 75 ft and the time taken in working twelve minutes. Entrance to the caissons was by guillotine gates and they submerged at the bottom of the plane. The installation was part of a belated effort to open up an all-wide route from London to Leicester and the east midlands by eliminating the narrow locks at Watford and Foxton. But traffic was never sufficiently heavy to justify the working expenses of the Foxton Lift and in addition there was trouble with the rails subsiding under the great weight of the caissons. The lift ceased work in 1910 and the machinery was dismantled in 1926.[20] Meanwhile, traffic reverted to the Foxton locks, while plans for widening the Watford locks were never proceeded with.

The history of the vertical canal lift is even less happy than that of the inclined plane. Obviously sites where such a lift could be placed in order to overcome a difference in level comparable with that of an inclined plane occurred very rarely. Hence they were advocated as a desirable substitute for locks, promising from twice to three times the fall of a single lock with great economy in the use of water. Their use in this way, however, meant that each lift could not be supervised. They were intended, like locks, to be worked by the boatmen themselves but their mechanism, without exception, proved too complex and unreliable to be operated in this way however much promise they might show when demonstrated by their proud inventors.

A lift was designed by John Woodhouse for the Worcester &
Birmingham canal as a more economical alternative to locks on the
long descent to the Severn. A prototype was, as we have seen, installed experimentally at Tardebigge, on the site of the present top lock,
in 1809 and tested in the following year. It had a fall of 14 ft and
consisted of a wooden caisson, capable of floating a single narrow
boat, connected by chains and overhead pulleys to counterweights
consisting of wooden boxes loaded with bricks. The out-of-balance
effect of the heavy suspension chains was counteracted by hanging
similar chains from the bottoms of the caisson and the counterweight
boxes on the principle of the trail rope of a balloon. In this way a
single winch was sufficient to operate the lift. There were guillotine
gates at each end of the caisson and at the upper end of the caisson
pit. After the lift had been tested for six months, the canal company
decided in favour of locks.

Instead of a dead weight, as at Tardebigge, it was manifestly
better to substitute a second caisson working in a parallel pit, as in
this case the lift could be made self-acting by adding more water to
the descending caisson. It is strange that Woodhouse did not adopt
such a design since it appears to have been first suggested by Dr
Anderson of Edinburgh in his book[21] published in 1794. Although
they varied in detail, the lifts designed by James Green for the Grand
Western and the Chard canals, by James Fussell for the Dorset &
Somerset and by Sir William Congreve for the Regent's Canal, all
worked on the principle proposed by Anderson.

The eight lifts at Taunton, Norton, Allerford, Hillfarrance, Nyne-
head, Winsbeer and Greenham on the Grand Western were the only
ones to work in day-to-day service, which they did for more than
thirty years, but only after considerable teething troubles had been
overcome. The lifts varied from as little as 12 ft 6 in at Norton to as
much as 42 ft 6 in in the case of the summit lift at Greenham. Power
to operate the lifts was obtained by adding two inches, or approximately one ton, of water to the upper caisson. At first a shallow lock
had to be provided at the foot of each lift because the level of water
in the caisson when it was lowered into the water in the bottom of
the lift pit would not equalize with that in the lower pound of the
canal. Green later cured this trouble by a method of forcing the
caisson against the lower gate and so excluding water from the pit.

The lift constructed by James Fussell at Mells differed from

Green's designs in that the tub boats were suspended in 'dry' cradles, power being provided by running water into a chamber below the upper cradle. It is difficult to see how boats could have been transferred from the upper canal into a dry cradle except by the method which Fulton proposed and illustrated in his book.[22] This consisted in floating the boat into a wheeled caisson. This caisson was then emptied into a side pond and propelled forward by rack and pinion gear to leave the boat suspended in its cradle over the lift pit. In the event of what Fulton calls 'a descending trade', the weight of a descending boat raised an empty one and at the same time worked pumps which returned the water from the side pond to the summit pound. For alternating trade, Fulton proposed a single lift on the same principle but powered by a descending bucket filled from the side pond.

In the case of Sir William Congreve's lift, one of which was built by Henry Maudslay and Co. and installed experimentally on the Regent's canal at Camden Town, the two caissons, in which full-sized boats were floated, were moved manually with the assistance of 'hydro-pneumatic' pressure. There was a communicating culvert between the two lift pits at the bottom so that the pressure of the descending caisson helped to raise its neighbour. This is said to have been achieved by 'compressed air trapped beneath the water',[23] though it is difficult to see how this could have been achieved and it is more probable that the device must have relied on hydraulic pressure alone. Even so, the caissons must have fitted their pits as snugly as a piston in a cylinder, otherwise the operation of the lift would have been attended with spectacular and alarming results. Not surprisingly, the experiment was unsuccessful.

Two attempts were made to harness a different principle to the problem of moving canal boats from one level to another without loss of water, that of the buoyancy of a completely enclosed and watertight caisson. Such was the principle of the experimental lift designed and patented by Messrs Rowland and Pickering of Ruabon and built by them on the Ellesmere canal. It was intended for use on the Pont Cysyllte–Chester section of the canal which was never completed. The whereabouts of the experiment are not known, but as boats were presumably used, it may have been on the site of the present double lock at Frankton.

It consisted of a lift pit sunk as far below the lower level of the canal as the lift intended, in this case 12 ft, and filled with water. In this pit was the closed caisson, supporting on iron columns 12 ft above it an open caisson large enough to float a narrow boat. Since the buoyancy of the lower caisson exactly equalled the weight of the upper one, the lift could be operated by one man using a simple winch. The idea was patented in 1794 and the experiment, witnessed by Jessop and Rennie, took place in 1796. It failed, though modern lifts on the Continent employ the same principle.

The most alarming of all canal lifts was that designed and built by Robert Weldon on the Somerset Coal Canal at Combe Hay, also in 1796. This operated on the same buoyancy principle, but in this case the narrow boat and its crew actually floated into a huge watertight caisson. This was permanently submerged in an awesome masonry pit 88 ft deep, 88 ft long and 20 ft wide at the centre, tapering to 11 ft 6 in at each end. Both the upper and lower canal approaches to the pit were in tunnels closed by gates, the operating lift being 46 ft. In Weldon's patent specification drawing,[24] the caisson is shown rectangular in section but, according to Chapman, it was cylindrical, which sounds more probable. As to how this monstrous device operated I cannot do better than quote Chapman's contemporary description:[25]

The caisson, or chest, is cylindric; and, in this instance, of sufficient strength to bear the pressure of a column of water 54 ft, or upwards; to which it is subjected, when opposite the lower level, on account of the necessity of its being covered when opposed to the entrance of the upper level. It is so balanced that when it has sufficient water within it to float a boat, it is of the same specific gravity as the medium it floats in: and, like an air balloon, it ascends or descends by a slight increase, or diminution of, its relative gravity; which, in this machine, is done by raising out, or admitting an inconsiderable quantity of water. The pit, in which the diving chest moves, has, opposite each level of canal, a tunnel or opening closed with gates; and is so much higher than the upper Canal as to contain a height of water just sufficient, as already mentioned, to cover the caisson when opposite the upper level. In this, or in its lower position, when run close to, and abutting against, the entrance, it is retained by the water being let out of the short part of the tunnel between the gates of the level, and the end of the caisson. It is then held there by the pressure of the column of water intervening between the surface of the pit and that of the Canal to which it is opposed. The gates of the level and Canal are then opened, and the boat goes in or out; and, on the gates being again closed, and the water let in to the vacancy, the diving chest is ready to proceed to the other level.

This description begs a lot of questions. For instance how was that 'inconsiderable quantity of water' 'raised out' of the caisson, as it lay at the bottom level, to enable it to ascend? In the technical competence of the time, it suggests a great deal of hard work with a hand operated force pump! Nevertheless, we are told that the lift worked experimentally, and we can but salute the intrepid boating party who, with infinite faith in the genius of Mr Weldon, submitted themselves to be imprisoned in his 'cassoon lock' as in a sunken submarine. Failure of the lift was due to the yielding of the masonry of the caisson pit under pressure from the surrounding earth. This is not surprising.

Vertical canal lifts became extinct in England with the closure of the Grand Western canal in 1864 until 1875 when the Anderton lift at Northwich was opened to traffic. At Anderton the Trent & Mersey canal passes at a height of 50 ft directly above the Weaver Navigation. It is almost the only situation in England where so considerable and steep a fall between two navigable waterways occurs naturally and it was thus peculiarly favourable to a lift. In 1809, Telford sent to Count Von Platen in Sweden a drawing of 'A Machine for raising vessels out of the river Weaver at Northwich'[26] and in 1813 an inclined plane railway was in use at this point.[27] Credit for the idea of the present vertical lift is due to Sir E. Leader Williams,* who was engaged in carrying out improvements on the Weaver Navigation at this time. But for the actual design of the lift, Edwin Clark was responsible and it was built by Emmerson, Murgatroyd and Co. Ltd.[28]

It consists of two caissons, each capable of floating a pair of narrow boats, moving vertically in a massive iron framework. Communicating gates are of the guillotine type. As originally built, the lift was

* Leader Williams was also responsible for the remarkable swing aqueduct at Barton which replaced the first Barton aqueduct when the Manchester Ship Canal was built.

counterbalanced, each caisson being supported on vertical hydraulic rams. By the end of the nineteenth century, however, trouble was being experienced owing to the 'grooving' of the rams due to electrolytic action caused by pollution of the water by a nearby chemical works.[29] In 1908 it was decided to convert the lift to electrical operation, each caisson being balanced independently by counterweights as on John Woodhouse's lift at Tardebigge, and in this form it survives to this day. It is the lone survivor in this country of a device over which so many ingenious men cudgelled their brains in times past with so little success.

CHAPTER TEN

Traffic and Motive Power

In pre-canal days, traffic on our navigable rivers was handled almost exclusively by gangs of men called bow-hauliers. They were aided by the current when travelling downstream, or by the wind. Most river barges carried sail, the Yorkshire Keels being the last craft in Britain to carry a square rig. Norfolk wherries trading on the Broads and associated rivers relied upon sail alone, owing to the flat nature of the country, and had an ingenious arrangement of counter-weighted mast and rigging which could be quickly lowered when passing under a low bridge. Unlike most river barges, wherries were not flat bottomed and had a keel. 'Slip keel wherries' were those fitted with a detachable keel which could be removed for working up the North Walsham & Dilham Canal. When the wind failed, wherries were laboriously propelled by means of a long pole called a 'quant'.

When bow-hauling a river barge, the tow line was attached at, or near, the top of the mast, because the banks along which the hauliers walked were often high and it was necessary to keep the line clear of the sallies that grew along the river's margin. Evidence of this may be seen on the famous iron bridge over the Severn at Coalbrookdale, where grooves worn by the towlines may be seen high up on the iron arch. Where, as in the case of the iron bridge, there was no clear towpath under the arch a barge proceeding up stream would have to make fast while the free end of the towline was dropped over the upstream side of the bridge and allowed to float down to the barge on the current, there to be secured. The other end could then be detached and towing continued.

Sometimes it was necessary for the bow-hauliers to cross the river by ferries and many river ferries were established primarily for this purpose, their use continuing when horses superseded men for towing. On many rivers, this change came late and under pressure from interested canal companies against the resistance of the bow-hauliers. It was not until 1804, for example, that a horse towing-path was provided on the lower Severn by the Gloucester & Worcester Horse Towing-Path Company. The change was welcomed by local land-owners who regarded the bow-hauliers, like the gypsies, as inveterate predators. In 1856 Henry Robinson[1] recorded that: 'The traffic on the Upper Thames was in the last century principally conducted by large barges carrying as much as 200 tons each, and hauled against the stream by 12–14 horses or 50–80 men; these men were usually of the worst possible character, and a terror to the whole neighbourhood of the river.'

The River Avon Navigation from Stratford down to Tewkesbury never had a horse towing-path, bow-hauling on the lower river persisting until the coming of steam power.

Throughout the hey-day of canals, horse towage was universal over the whole system, though sometimes mules were preferred as being more hardy, while on the canals associated with the Severn pairs of donkeys were preferred for the same reason. On the narrow canals, one horse or mule to one boat was usually the rule, although sometimes one would pull two boats. In that case it was necessary for the crew to bow-haul the second boat down a flight of narrow locks. The tow line was attached to a metal stud or 'luby' fixed to the top of a squat 'mast' set in the forepart of the boat. This mast was telescopic, the solid central portion sliding in a lower portion of box section and being adjustable by means of holes and a removable cross pin.

A horse had to exert its greatest effort in starting a loaded boat moving out of a narrow lock, and to do this it had to be trained to 'hang in the collar'. Here again, mules were generally better at this than horses. To assist the horse in this task a simple device was used to provide a two-to-one purchase. A swivel (pulley) was attached to the stud on the mast. The towing line, which was provided with a loop and a wooden cross piece or stop at the boat end, was run through this pulley and the loop slipped over a stud set in the masonry of the lock wing-wall. The horse thus obtained a two-to-one purchase until the mast of the boat drew level with the stud on the lock wall when the loop slipped off the latter allowing the line to run through the pulley until checked by the wooden stop, when direct haulage was resumed.

Where, as often happens, the tow path changes sides it was

necessary for the horse to cross the canal and for this purpose special
'turnover bridges' were usually provided, carrying the towpath both
over and under the bridge to avoid the necessity for detaching the
towline.

In passing through long tunnels, where there was a towing path,
or over high aqueducts, horses had to be specially trained. For
example, on the section of the Shropshire Union canal that includes
Chirk tunnel and the aqueducts at Chirk and Pont Cysyllte, young
horses were usually blindfolded until they had become accustomed
to the job.

Before the coming of railways, passenger 'packet boats' were
operated on many canals. These were of finer build than the normal
trading boat to enable them to travel faster in a channel of restricted
width. These were usually towed by two horses and there was no
central mast, the lines from the two horses being attached to
'timber-heads' at bow and stern. A postillion usually rode the hinder
of the two horses. The last of these craft to survive was the Bridgewater Canal packet boat *Duchess Countess*. Having been sunk in her
home waters for many years, she was salvaged and taken to the
Shropshire Union canal near Frankton where she was used as a
houseboat for many years. Latterly, she had to be drawn out of the
water and she finally disintegrated in the 1950s.

The last canal in Britain over which regular passenger services (as
opposed to pleasure trips) operated was the Gloucester & Berkeley on
which the Gloucester & Berkeley Steam Packet Company operated a
service. In 1935 this was advertised as conveying 'passengers and goods,
twice daily each way in summer, calling at intermediate stations'.[2]

When two horsedrawn boats met, one boatman had to 'give way'
to the other by dropping his line in the water so that the oncoming
boat could float over it. To those who have witnessed this procedure
in the comparatively recent past it appears a simple and leisurely
operation. They can have no conception of the confusion and bad
language so caused in the past by the constant meeting of boats on
canals carrying a heavy traffic which was entirely horse-hauled.
There was—officially at any rate—a strict order of priority, mineral
carrying boats giving way to boats carrying parcels or general
merchandise and both to passenger boats. The *Duchess Countess*
carried on her bow a scimitar-shaped knife * to cut the towline of any

* Now preserved in the Waterways Museum, Stoke Bruerne.

boat that failed to give way to her. Because of this passing difficulty and the confusion so caused, a contemporary hailed Telford's arrangement of two towing paths on the reconstructed Birmingham Canal main line as the greatest single improvement made in canals since their inception.

The right of first passage through a lock was often hotly disputed by the captains of boats approaching from opposite directions. On heavily used canals an effort was made to eliminate this source of friction by erecting posts at an equal distance from the lock in both directions and by instituting the rule that the boat first past a post should have the lock. So far as is known, this system was first introduced on the Grand Junction canal. A variant of it was subsequently used on the single line of the Stockton & Darlington Railway to determine who should go forward and who back to the nearest passing loop.

Mention has already been made of the delays caused to traffic by the early tunnels where there was no alternative to the slow and laborious process of 'legging' the boats through. In the early days, the boatmen lay on their sides on either end of a plank thrown across the boat and pushed with their feet against the tunnel walls. This was extremely hazardous since an incautious movement by one man could easily throw the other off and many were drowned in this way. In the short Tardebigge tunnel alone, the parish registers record that three men were drowned in 1842 and two more, within a week of each other, in 1846.[3] Eventually safer boards called 'wings', which hooked onto the boat, were introduced.

In the case of long 'legging' tunnels passing a heavy traffic professional 'leggers' were employed to work the boats through. At Blisworth, for example, there were two gangs of twelve men each stationed at either end of the tunnel, four out of each gang taking night duty. Two of their numbered brass armbands, which proclaimed that they were registered as professional leggers by the Grand Junction company, may be seen in the Waterways Museum at Stoke Bruerne.

Because of its length combined with exceptionally heavy traffic, Blisworth Tunnel presented a particularly acute problem. At first, continuous wooden 'slide rails' were provided along the side walls 6 in below water level and wooden chocks were fixed above this rail at 9 ft intervals to serve as a purchase so that boats could be 'shafted' through. But this must have been as dangerous and tedious an operation as legging and the rails and chocks soon disappeared. In 1869 a system of haulage by endless wire rope driven by stationary steam engines was installed in both Blisworth and Braunston Tunnels, but this was evidently not satisfactory for in 1871 it was replaced by a regular service of steam tugs.

Tunnel towage was the first service to which mechanical traction was regularly applied on the canals, but where steam tugs were used it raised the problem of ventilation. A slow-moving tug and its tow does not have the self-ventilating effect of a train in a railway tunnel, and in the longer tunnels the introduction of tugs meant that old working shafts had to be opened up as ventilation shafts. Even so, the atmsophere in Blisworth and Braunston tunnels in steam tug days was apt to be impenetrable and scarcely breathable as this writer can recall only too vividly.

At Harecastle new tunnel, where the problem of ventilation was acute, a solution was found in an electric tug which hauled itself along on a steel cable laid in the bed of the canal. This was introduced in 1914, the towing path through the tunnel having become unusable owing to mining subsidence. Originally, it was supplied with current from batteries in two 'tender' boats, one of which was always being charged at a small generating station at the south end of the tunnel. In 1920 it was converted to a tram-type pick-up from an overhead cable. All boats, powered or otherwise, were compelled to use this tug which therefore remained in service until 1954 when it was withdrawn and special ventilating equipment installed.

Services of steam tugs, running to timetable operated through most of the busier canal tunnels until the end of the era of horse haulage. They worked through Preston Brook, Barnton and Saltersford tunnels on the Trent & Mersey, Foulridge and Gannow tunnels on the Leeds & Liverpool (where the tugs had propellers at each end to avoid the necessity for turning round), Westhill, Shortwood, and Tardebigge tunnels on the Worcester & Birmingham canal, and Islington and Maida Hill tunnels on the Regent's Canal. These services mostly ceased during the 1930s when horse boats finally gave way to self-propelled craft. With the exception of the Regent's Canal where tugs are still used for towing dumb barges from the Thames, tugs survived longest on the Worcester & Birmingham canal where they continued to tow horsedrawn narrow boats through the tunnels until after the last war. A compound condensing steam tug built by Abdela, Mitchell and Co., of Brimscombe worked this service through Westhill tunnel until 1942 when its boiler was condemned and the surviving Bollinder-engined tug then worked the boats through all three tunnels.

So that they could be towed in 'trains' through tunnels, horse-boats were equipped with 'tunnel hooks' fitted on either side of the stern in order to keep the towline clear of the tall rudder post or 'ram's head'. There was on the Grand Junction canal a considerable trade in explosives to Weedon Military Depot, which had its own canal basin. Boatmen engaged in this trade were forbidden to use the tunnel tugs; the boats had to be 'legged' through. This precaution followed the disaster of 1874 on the Regents Canal, when the boat *Tilbury*, one of a train in tow behind a steam tug and loaded with gunpowder, blew up as it was passing under Macclesfield bridge, Regent's Park, with spectacularly destructive results.

In the case of short tunnels where there was no towing path, a chain was often hung along the wall so that boatmen could haul themselves through or, where this was not provided, they used shafts. With the exception of explosive traffic, the ancient practice of legging survived longest on those canals where long tunnels were combined with a light traffic which never justified the use of tugs. Such a one was the Leicester Line, as it is now called, the old Grand Union and Old Union canals. Here, if they were not lucky enough to obtain a tow from a passing motor-boat, occasional horsedrawn coal boats continued to leg through the tunnels at Crick, Husbands Bosworth and Saddington until just before the last war.

To judge from contemporary prints, the earliest narrow boats evolved from the 'starvationers' of the Bridgewater Canal were crudely constructed craft with a straight stem carrying only a small cabin aft, or none at all. They resembled the 'Day Boats' or 'Joey Boats' of which great numbers were in use until recently for short-haul traffic on the Birmingham canal system. The resemblance is logical, for traffic on the first canals was preponderantly local. Canal companies were only toll collectors, being forbidden to carry in their own boats, but as the canal system expanded into something resembling a national network, so a long distance carrying trade was born and firms such as Pickfords came into being. It was in the boatbuilding yards of such firms, it would seem, that the long distance narrow boat as we know it was born.

On the evidence of contemporary prints, these long distance craft owned by carrying companies displayed none of the elaborate decorations, the roses and castles, such as we associate with the narrow boat today. The earliest depiction of such decoration that this writer has seen dates from 1875. The early carrying company's boats appear to have been manned by all male crews, who could afford to house their families ashore, and it was not until railway competition brought hard times to the canals that the boatman was compelled to take his wife and family on to the boat with him. Pictorial evidence certainly seems to support the belief that this move was the starting point of elaborate decoration and that it does not pre-date the coming of railway competition.

Mention has already been made of canals which were built to suit existing local types of river craft, the Yorkshire Keel canals being the most extensive example. On some other canals not closely linked with the narrow canal system, special types of boat were evolved. The Leeds & Liverpool canal evolved its own type of 'short boat' differing from the Keel and measuring 62 ft long by 14 ft 3 in beam, carrying 45 tons on a draught of 3 ft 9 in. On the canals of South Wales, boats generally shorter but broader in the beam than the narrow boat were used. Their dimensions varied slightly from 65 ft by 7 ft 6 in on the Swansea Canal to 60 ft by 9 ft on the Neath Canal. Their average load was 20 tons. Since they were used for short haul traffic, few carried cabins and most were 'double ended', the rudder being transferable from one end to the other. After the closure of these Welsh canals, some of them found their way across the Bristol Channel and for many years could be seen doing duty as maintenance boats on the Kennet & Avon Canal.

Fen lighters that used to work on the small drainage waterways of the Bedford Level operated in 'gangs' of five, close coupled together by chains. The same method was adopted on a smaller scale on the tub boat canals of Shropshire and the west of England, as many as twenty boats being towed by one horse, the boatman in charge keeping the foremost boat in the centre of the channel with the aid of a long shaft from the towpath. The tub boats used on the Bude Canal measured 20 ft by 5 ft 6 in, loading 4 tons on a draught of 1 ft 8 in. Shropshire tub boats were slightly larger and carried 5 tons. Whereas it was the practice in the west of England to use a boat with a wedge-shaped bow at the head of a tub boat train, all the Shropshire tub boats were uncompromisingly rectangular. The oblong iron boxes known as compartment boats or 'Tom Puddings', used with such success in the heavy coal trade on the Aire & Calder Navigation, represent a latter day application of the tub boat principle. Each box measures 20 ft by 16 ft and loads 35 tons on a draught of 6 ft. The old method of working these compartment boats was to push them in front of a tug, steering the train by wire ropes passing down each side, but it was superseded by the more normal method of towage. They followed west country tub boat practice by using a short wedge-shaped boat, known as a 'Dummy Bows' at the head of the train. By means of special hydraulic hoists at Goole Docks, these compartment boats could be discharged directly into steamers.

During the period when the Grand Junction canal was building and for a few years thereafter, the talk in canal circles was all of a system of barge canals throughout the country and of widening existing canals to the broad gauge. The Grand Junction company was very active in promoting or supporting such schemes. Initially, the Grand Junction was used by wide boats, as was from the first intended, and as late as 1831 Priestley had this to say of it: 'The navigation of this canal is used by barges, square at head and stern, and having flat bottoms, of sixty tons burthen, and smaller vessels of twenty-five tons burthen, with sharp heads and sterns.'[4] These barges, assuming Priestley was correct, must have been 'swim-headed' like the lighters used today on London River, a somewhat unwieldy choice for canal navigation one would have thought. The smaller craft referred to are obviously narrow boats and evidently the Grand Junction company discovered that for long distance work they were far more suitable. A pair of them could load almost as much as one barge, travel more easily in a restricted channel than a barge, pass through broad locks together, and present no passing problem in tunnels or bridges. Moreover, they could travel to or from any point on the Midlands canal system without the need for transhipment. This transhipment factor was probably decisive in killing the wide boat in the same way that, on the railways, it killed Brunel's broad gauge. Certainly the Grand Junction company abandoned its campaign for a system of broad waterways; so much so that the Grand Union canal which, as we have seen, was largely Grand Junction promoted, was built with narrow locks at Watford and Foxton.

It is true that de Salis, writing in 1904, refers to wide boats, of a size intermediate between a narrow boat and a barge, being in use on the Grand Junction. These were from 70 ft to 72 ft long by from 10 ft to 11 ft beam and loaded 50 tons on a draught of 4 ft, but their use was doubtless mainly confined to the lower part of the main line where, down to modern times, barge traffic has plied between the Thames and the paper mills at Watford and King's Langley.

The fact that history repeats itself is due to man's failure to learn from it. When the Grand Union Canal Company was formed in 1929 by the amalgamation of the Grand Junction, Regent's and the two Warwick Companies, the dream of operating wide boats between London and Birmingham took on a new lease of life and to this end all the Warwick locks were widened and much deepening and widening work was done throughout. But only one prototype craft, the *Progress* of 66 tons burden, was ever built, and when the Grand Union Canal Carrying Company was later formed, after a brief experiment with compartment boats, narrow boats were chosen for the new fleet.

For the purpose of calculating the tonnage tolls payable, all canal boats had to be 'gauged' by toll clerks stationed at strategic points on the system. On the narrow canals where boats were all of the same type, this presented little difficulty. When a new boat was built, she was sent to a special 'Weigh Dock' such as that beside the Grand Junction canal near the north end of Braunston tunnel. Here she would be progressively loaded with weights while the displacement in inches per ton fore and aft was accurately measured. Sometimes, as on the Shropshire Union, appropriately calibrated scales were then fixed to the boat's sides, but more usually the information was sent to the toll clerks concerned to be recorded in their books. The clerks then measured the displacement with a calibrated gauging rod and ascertained the tonnage from their boat record.

On a canal which handled different types of craft, this system broke down. Such was the case in the hey-day of the Thames & Severn Canal where a barge trading down the Upper Thames, a narrow 'fly boat' working through from Gloucester to London via the Wilts & Berks canal, or one of the smaller Severn trows with a cargo of salt for Lechlade might successively present themselves at Brimscombe Port. This situation defeated the company's toll clerk there and was soon exploited by unscrupulous traders. One of the company's agents then suggested a dock at Brimscombe in which any suspected vessel might be weighed, and a model of this device was approved by the canal committee. It consisted of a dry dock in which, when the water had been let out, the vessel was left resting upon the iron pan of what was, in effect, a gigantic steelyard. The original model of this device is now in the Gloucester Folk Museum, while the dock became a swimming pool. In the first year of operation this machine detected overweight cargo to the tune of £1,154 in extra tolls, which more than covered the cost of its construction.[5] This was in contrast to the sad later years of this canal when 'lightening boats' had to be provided at each end of Sapperton Tunnel owing to the chronic shortage of water on the summit. A boatman would offload part of his cargo into the lightening boat and then tow it behind him as he legged his way through the tunnel.[6]

The spread of canals in England coincided with the development of the steam engine, so it is not surprising that the idea of using steam power as a means of canal boat propulsion was canvassed at a very early date. Appropriately enough, the first two canals to be built became the scene of the earliest experiments in steam propulsion.

Of the Sankey Canal (St Helens), Priestley[7] wrote: 'An experiment of propelling vessels by steam was tried upon this canal as early as 1797, when a loaded barge was worked up and down by a steam engine on board for a distance of twenty miles; but, singular as it may appear, to this time (1831) vessels have continued to be towed by manual power.' Priestley got the date wrong. The experiment was made in June 1793, only five years after Symington's and Miller's famous experiment on Dalswinton Loch, Dumfries, and the author of it was a certain John Smith of St Helens, who was described as 'an uneducated mechanic'.[8] The hull of the boat was purchased in Liverpool and the machinery installed by Smith at St Helens with the financial help of Thomas Baldwin. Because of the Watt patent monopoly, the single cylinder was of the open-topped Newcomen 'atmospheric' type and drove side paddle wheels, each having seven floats, by a beam and connecting rod. It is said to have achieved a speed of two miles an hour at eighteen strokes a minute. Later, this steamboat crossed the Mersey to Runcorn and steamed up the Bridgewater Canal to Manchester. To those who ridiculed his contraption, Smith is said to have replied: 'Before twenty years are over, you will see this river covered with smoke.'[9] He was not far wrong.

On 5 November 1794 a meeting of the Mersey & Irwell Navigation Company's Board minuted: 'A person in Liverpool having produced to the Committee a model of a boat navigated by Machinery . . . Mr Wright was directed to pay him five guineas.'[10] The recipient of this largesse was almost certainly John Smith.

Whereas the 'Old Navigators', true to form, took no further action, the Duke of Bridgewater was keenly interested and resolved to repeat the experiment. At about this time he was introduced by the Duke of Devonshire to Robert Fulton, fresh from his deliberations about tub boat canals with Lord Stanhope in Cornwall, and under Fulton's direction a second steamer was built for the Bridgewater Canal. The machinery was supplied by J. and T. Sherratt, engineers of Salford, but the hull and paddlewheels were built in the Duke's yard at Worsley.[11] It is on record that, at this time, a firm known as Bateman and Sherrat were building for the Lancashire cotton mills engines in which two Newcomen type cylinders drove an overhead rocking shaft by toothed racks on their piston rods and gearwheels. Rotary motion was derived from this rocking shaft by cranks and connecting rods.[12] It is safe to assume that the engine used in the boat was of this type as it would offer advantages over the more orthodox beam engine as used by Smith.

Apparently this steamboat succeeded in drawing a train of eight 25 ton coal boats, close coupled on the tub boat principle, from Worsley to Manchester at a speed of one mile an hour. After Fulton's departure to Paris in 1797, the experiments were continued by Captain Shanks R.N. of Deptford, but in 1799 they were abandoned. The steamboat was christened *Buonaparte* by the Bridgewater Canal boatmen, from which one may gather that it was decidedly unpopular with them. Its engine finished its career at one of the Duke's collieries where it became more affectionately known as 'Old Nancy' and worked until 1851.[13]

Such eighteenth-century experiments could not hope for more than a very limited success, because Boulton and Watt's Patent monopoly, coupled with their persistent refusal to co-operate in steam propulsion experiments of any kind, forced inventors to use the Newcomen principle which was inherently unsuitable for rotative motion. When the Watt Patent lapsed in 1800, aspiring inventors at last had an unfettered choice of motive power.

In 1801 William Symington built the famous stern-wheeled steam tug *Charlotte Dundas* for use on the Forth & Clyde Canal at the instance of Lord Dundas, the Governor of the canal. The details of this pioneer craft are well known and will not be repeated here. Suffice it that in March 1802 she towed two barges, each of 70 tons burden, for a distance of nineteen and a half miles along the canal in six hours against a strong head wind.[14] Nevertheless, the Forth & Clyde Company decided that the advantages of steam tugs did not compensate for the damage done to the canal banks by wash and the *Charlotte Dundas* was laid up. Symington's hopes were raised, however, when the Duke of Bridgewater ordered eight similar tugs for his canal. Unfortunately, the Duke died shortly afterwards and his order was repudiated by his agent, Captain Bradshaw. Poor Symington died in poverty, a disappointed man.

Because of the fear—by no means unfounded—which the Forth & Clyde company had expressed that steamboats would damage canal banks by their wash, it was on the wider waters of navigable rivers that steamboats first made headway. The River Hull has the distinction of being the first navigable waterway in England on which steam propulsion was tried out. Robert Fourness and James Ashworth of York built a small paddle driven steamboat which ran from Hull to Beverley in 1787. Three cylinders acting on a three-throw crankshaft drove side paddles having twenty radial floats. This little vessel was later conveyed to London where it ran trials on the Thames and is said to have been purchased by the Prince Regent as a pleasure boat. Soon afterwards it was burnt—by Thames watermen, it is supposed, fearing the new power.[15]

Matthew Murray fitted the captured French privateer *L'Actif* with one of Trevithick's high pressure engines in 1811–12 to the order of John Wright, a Yarmouth Quaker. Renamed *Experiment*, this steamer sailed to Yarmouth where she made her first voyage from Yarmouth to Braydon in August 1813. She later worked regularly between Yarmouth and Norwich.[16]

In 1814 steam tugs first worked between Hull and Gainsborough on the Trent[17] and between Gloucester and Worcester on the Severn.[18] Regular services started on both rivers a few years later.

It was the threat of railway competition that persuaded the canal companies to take a second look at the possibility of using steam power, and many fanciful schemes for 'canal trains' appeared at this

Scheme for 'canal train' of 1848

time. William Fairbairn carried out an elaborate series of experiments on the Forth & Clyde canal, both with horsedrawn boats and with the steam sternwheeler *Cyclops*, in which he studied the wash created by the boats at varying speeds. Fairbairn became an advocate of steam power for canals and, as a result of his experiments, the passenger steamer *Lord Dundas* was built for the Forth & Clyde by Fairbairn and Lillie of Manchester. She was a twin-hulled craft with a single central paddle wheel.

Faced with competition, canal companies pressed the government for power to act as carriers on their own canals. The Ellesmere & Chester canal company obtained its own act for this purpose in 1830, but this was followed by a general act in 1845. This measure undoubtedly stimulated the introduction of steam power, although at first this chiefly took the form of company owned tugs towing 'trains' of bye-traders' boats on canals which were not heavily locked. Steam tugs were introduced on the Aire & Calder Navigation in 1836 and on the Macclesfield and Shropshire Union canals in the 1840s. On the last named, tugs at first operated between Autherley Junction and Ellesmere Port, but later their use was confined to the section between Chester and the Port. Steam tugs were regularly employed on the Gloucester & Berkeley from 1860 onwards, and on the Bridgewater Canal from 1874.

The railway companies, taking advantage of the undoubted damage caused to the banks by the wash of power driven craft, banned steamers on all canals owned by them. In 1856 the steam tug *Pioneer*, designed by John Inshaw of Birmingham with twin contra-rotating propellers to minimize wash, was bought by the Moira Colliery Co. for towing boats on the long level of the Ashby Canal.[19] The owners of the canal, the Midland Railway Company, prohibited its use, but this prohibition was successfully contested in the Court of

Chancery following experiments conducted by an independent engineer which showed that provided speed did not exceed three miles an hour, no injurious breaking wave was created. Following this victory additional tugs, the *Volunteer* and the *Harrison* were commissioned, and these towed coal boats from Ashby to Coventry, Rugby, and Braunston.

Owing to the wash created by propellers, various alternative methods of mechanical haulage were tried during the nineteenth century. An experiment with cable haulage was made on the Bridgewater Canal and electrical traction, using overhead supply cables, on a section of the Staffordshire & Worcestershire Canal. Through the agency of its parent, the London and North-Western Railways, the Shropshire Union experimented with steam locomotive haulage on its Middlewich branch in 1888. Eighteen-inch gauge metals were laid along the towpath and the small four-wheeled locomotives were designed especially by John Ramsbottom and built at Crewe. The experiment was soon abandoned, but the locomotives were put to work on an internal railway in Crewe works. The actual locomotives used in the experiment have been scrapped, but one of similar type is now preserved in the Narrow Gauge Railway Museum at Towyn.

All the earlier applications of steam power on canals appear to have been used solely for towage and so far as is known the first use of steam cargo carrying craft was on the Grand Junction Canal in the 1860s. These steam boats were operated by the canal company and although no details of them are known, since each operated with a towed 'butty' boat, we may assume that they were narrow boats.

Latterly, the two most notable fleets of cargo-carrying steamers were those operated by the Leeds & Liverpool Canal Carrying Company and by the carrying firm of Fellows, Morton and Clayton on the Grand Junction and its associated waterways. Both originated about 1880.

The Leeds & Liverpool fleet totalled thirty craft. The hulls were of the normal 'short boat' design except that they were narrower in the beam, 13 ft instead of 14 ft 2 in. They loaded 28–30 tons, the machinery occupying ten tons of cargo space. They had Field boilers, as fitted to contemporary fire engines, which were very quick steaming. The engines, built by G. Wilkinson and Co. Ltd, of Wigan, were diagonal double tandem compounds, that is to say the high and low pressure cylinders were arranged in pairs, one above the other, sharing a common piston and connecting rod. Each engine consisted of two of these pairs arranged in Vee formation.

Curiously enough, these engines ran non-condensing as 'puffers'. One boat of the fleet, the *Leonora* was fitted with a jet condenser and ran an extended comparative trial with the 'puffer' *Amy*. As a result, the *Leonora* showed a slightly higher coal consumption so it was decided not to use condensers. A loaded steamer towing two loaded 'short boats', a total of about 110 tons, could travel the whole length of the Leeds & Liverpool main line, 127 miles and 92 locks, at an average speed of 2 mph, including the time spent in lockage. On such a journey the cost worked out at a little over one-tenth of a penny per ton mile, including fuel, men's wages, oil and engine stores, depreciation and interest on capital. The company maintained that this represented a saving of 25 per cent on the cost of the 300 horses which the steamers replaced.[20]

When the fleet was disbanded, many of the steamers were sold to bye-traders, a few of the steamers continuing in operation until the 1950s,[21] but the rest were fitted with Widdop Diesel engines which were locally built at Keighley.

The Fellows, Morton and Clayton steamers were narrow boats of 'composite' construction, that is to say they had elm bottoms but iron sides. A horizontal return-tube boiler, 6 ft long and 4 ft in diameter, supplied steam at 140 lb p.s.i. to a two-cylinder vertical tandem compound engine with cylinders 5 in and 10 in diameter by 10 in stroke. These engines were built by A. H. Beasley and Co. of Uxbridge. Unlike the Leeds & Liverpool steamers, they ran condensing and burned coke. They were always kept in a highly polished and spotless condition, a curtain (supplied by the owners) being hung between the boiler and the engine to protect the latter from dust.

A steamer and its towed 'butty' was manned by an all male crew of seven, immaculate in white overalls and white cord trousers. They worked 'fly', that is to say twenty four-hours a day, to a strict time-table and time keeping was so exemplary that a crew could estimate to a quarter of a mile where they would meet a boat scheduled in the opposite direction. It is said that they could run for eight miles or more without firing and a hammock was slung in the engine room so that the fireman could rest in between times.

The usual London terminus of these steamers was the City Road Basin, but from this starting point they worked on four different turns. Many ran only to Braunston because of the narrow locks beyond this point. At a depot* at Braunston the steamer's cargo was offloaded into a butty boat which, together with the steamer's butty, was taken forward to Birmingham by horses. The steamer reloaded, picked up a loaded butty, and returned to London. The crews engaged on this turn were known as the 'Braunston Rubbing Rags'. Some cargoes, however, especially soap, were worked right through to Birmingham by the steamers, the crews on this run being known as the 'Greasy Wheelers' or 'Greasy Ockers'. The latter term probably derives from Ocker Hill, where Fellows, Morton and Clayton had their early headquarters. Crews working steamers to Coventry were known as the 'Mud Heelers', perhaps a cynical commentary on the state of the Oxford canal. Finally, there were the 'Woolly Backed 'Uns', those who worked the steamer service from London up the Leicester Section to Nottingham.[22] The origin of this name is obscure unless it refers to the wool trade of Leicestershire.

The machinery on these steam narrow boats occupied ten tons of cargo space, and before the first world war Fellows, Morton and Clayton had begun to replace them by the much more compact Swedish single-cylinder Bollinder direct reversing semidiesel engine, thereby making available an extra five tons of cargo space. The last steamer travelled through the Grand Junction in 1931 and was abandoned at Hillmorton on the Oxford canal.

Diesel propelled motor-boats, each towing a 'butty', thus became the invariable form of transportation on the narrow canal system, although on some narrow canals motor-boats worked singly. The all-steel boats having full diesel engines and marine gearboxes built for the Grand Union Canal Carrying Company's fleet and those of the Severn & Canal Carrying Company represent the narrow boat in its final form. Some of the Severn boats were unusual in having the cabin accommodation arranged forward of the engine compartment.

No matter what form of propulsion may be used, ice is the greatest enemy of canal transport. The traditional form of icebreaker was a small iron boat having rounded bilges and equipped with a raised central rail, parallel with the keel. This was drawn forward by a team of horses while a gang of men, clinging to the rail, rocked the

* This depot stood on the right of the arm leading to Braunston Boatyard, the Boatyard being on the left. After standing empty and disused for many years it was demolished recently, the site now being used as a car park.

boat to and fro in order to break down the ice upon either side and so prevent the boat from becoming wedged. Latterly, powered tugs have been equipped as icebreakers although, in the worst conditions, it is doubtful if they are as effective as the older horsedrawn type. But a long spell of frost can defeat any icebreaker, for even if a channel can be kept clear, an accumulation of broken ice makes lockage well nigh impossible, jamming boats in the chambers and fouling the gates. Under such conditions, all movement may be stopped for weeks on end, and traffic thus lost to road or rail is not easily regained.

The arctic weather in the first two months of 1963 brought the surviving fleet of commercial craft on the narrow canals completely to a stand. This proved to be the *coup de grâce* and there is now practically no commercial traffic left on the whole of the narrow canal system apart from a few enthusiastic bye-traders. The harsh fact is that, under modern economic conditions, the pay load of the narrow boat is too small to justify the man hours expended in working it. Conversely, assuming these waterways were to be widened to admit boats of economic burden, it is extremely doubtful whether sufficient water would be available to work them.

Nevertheless, the narrow canal system, apart from being a monument to bygone engineering skill, is an asset which this country cannot afford to lose. As water suppliers to industry these canals are proving increasingly valuable, while they have been described as a linear National Park 2,000 miles long. As such they are an invaluable asset in this overcrowded island, a fact that the astonishingly rapid growth of pleasure traffic in the past decade demonstrates.

That the value of our narrow canal system has at last been recognized by government was shown by the White Paper published in September 1967. This proposes the retention of virtually the whole of the remaining system as an amenity. This means that posterity will enjoy the canals that the great engineers of the past have given us.

Source References

CHAPTER ONE

1 A. W. Skempton, 'The engineers of the English river navigations, 1620–1760', Newcomen Society *Transactions*, vol. 29,
1953, p. 25.

2 H. R. de Salis, *Handbook of Inland Navigation*, 1904 edn, p. 327.

3 See Brian Waters, *Severn Tide*, Dent 1947, for description and
illustration of putcheon weir.

4 See Arthur E. J. Went, 'Some ancient Irish salmon fishing
weirs', *Journal of Industrial Archaeology*, vol. 3, no. 3, 1966,
p. 153.

5 H. R. Robertson, *Life on the Upper Thames*, 1875, pp. 127–9.

6 Ronald H. Clark, 'The Staunches and Navigation of the Little
Ouse River', Newcomen Society *Transactions*, vol. 30, 1957,
p. 207.

7 H. R. Robertson, pp. 40–41.

8 H. R. de Salis, p. 13.

9 R. H. Clark.

10 A. W. Skempton, p. 38.

11 T. S. Willan, *River Navigation in England, 1600–1750*, 1936,
pp. 25–6 (2nd edn 1964).

12 *Ibid*, p. 26.

13 See F. S. Thacker, *The Thames Highway*, vol. 2, *Locks and
Weirs*, privately printed, 1920.

14 MS quoted by T. S. Willan, p. 97.

15 J. M. Palmer and M. I. Berrill, 'Andrew Yarranton and the
navigation works at Astley', *Journal* of the Railway and Canal
Historical Society, vol. 4, no. 3, 1958.

16 L. T. C. Rolt, *Inland Waterways of England*, Allen and Unwin,
1950, p. 33.

CHAPTER TWO

1 William Maitland, *History of London*, 1756 edn, quoted by A. W. Skempton to whom I am indebted for all information on John Hadley.
2 *The Diary of Ralph Thoresby*, F.R.S., 1830 edn, quoted by A. W. Skempton.
3 Joseph Priestley, *Historical Account of the Navigable Rivers, Canals and Railways throughout Great Britain*, 1831, pp. 475–8.
4 A. W. Skempton, to whom I am indebted for all information on Thomas Steers.
5 Joseph Priestley, p. 130.

CHAPTER THREE

1 R. H. Clark, discussion on his Paper, Newcomen Society *Transactions*, vol. 30, p. 217.
2 Joseph Priestley, p. 592.
3 *Ibid*, p. 97.
4 Hugh Malet, *The Canal Duke*, David and Charles 1961, p. 168.
5 Joseph Priestley, p. 100.
6 Hugh Malet.
7 Joseph Priestley, p. 97.
8 Hugh Malet, p. 104.
9 Samuel Smiles, *Lives of the Engineers*, vol. 1, 1862 edn, pp. 382–3.
10 Letter, Josiah Wedgwood to Thomas Bentley, quoted by Charles Hadfield, *Canals of the West Midlands*, David and Charles 1966, p. 29.
11 L. T. C. Rolt, *Thomas Telford*, Longmans 1958, p. 164.
12 See Charles Hadfield, *Canals of the East Midlands*, David and Charles 1966, chapter 1 deals with the early history of the Coventry and Oxford canal projects.
13 Oxford Canal Minute Book, quoted by Hadfield, *ibid*.
14 H. Thorpe, 'The Lord and the landscape', Birmingham Arch. Soc. *Transactions*, 1962, p. 71.
15 Charles Hadfield, *Canals of the East Midlands*, p. 22.

CHAPTER FOUR

1 Joseph Priestley, p. 134.
2 *Ibid*, p. 249.

3 Information supplied by Mr Charles Hadfield following a study of the company's minute books.

4 See *Personal Recollections of English Engineers, etc.* which Conder published anonymously in 1868.

5 Joseph Priestley, p. 15.

6 C. T. G. Boucher, *Life of John Rennie*, Manchester U.P. 1963, pp. 46–8.

7 H. R. de Salis, *Handbook*, p. 314.

8 Joseph Priestley, p. 579.

9 C. T. G. Boucher, p. 88.

CHAPTER FIVE

1 I am indebted to Dr C. T. G. Boucher for this translation.

2 For an account of this tramway and others mentioned in this book, see B. Baxter, *Stone Blocks and Iron Rails*, David and Charles 1966.

3 Joseph Priestley, p. 408.

4 See Charles Hadfield, *Canals of the West Midlands*, pp. 170–3, for a statement of this point of view.

5 Thomas Telford, *Life*, ed. John Rickman, 1838.

6 Charles Hadfield, *Canals of the West Midlands*, p. 163.

7 Charles Hadfield, *Canals of South Wales and the Border*, David and Charles 1960, p. 114.

8 For a full account of this historic event see H. W. Dickinson and A. Titley, *Richard Trevithick*, Cambridge U.P. 1934.

CHAPTER SIX

1 Charles Hadfield, *Canals of the West Midlands*.

2 H. R. de Salis, *Handbook*, p. 15.

3 Joseph Priestley, p. 333.

4 Information supplied by C. N. Hadlow.

5 For a complete account of this tramway see Victor A. Hatley, 'The Blisworth Hill Railway, 1800–1805', Northants Antiquarian Soc. *Papers*, 1962–63.

6 See Charles Hadfield, *Canals of the East Midlands*, pp. 85–9 for a complete account of this abortive canal/tramway project.

7 See L. T. C. Rolt, *George and Robert Stephenson*, Longmans 1960, pp. 240–1.

CHAPTER SEVEN

1 Thomas Telford, *Life*.
2 See L. T. C. Rolt, *Thomas Telford* for a more detailed account of the building of the B. & L.J. and the trouble with Shelmore.
3 Charles Hadfield, *Canals of the West Midlands*, p. 211.

CHAPTER EIGHT

1 Joseph Priestley, p. 437.
2 R. C. Gaut, *A History of Worcestershire Agriculture and Rural Evolution*, Worcester, Littlebury 1939, p. 199.
3 I Cohen, 'The Leominster-Stourport Canal', Woolhope Club *Transactions*, vol. 25, 1955–57.
4 Charles Hadfield, *Canals of Southern England*, Phoenix House 1955, p. 88.
5 Robin Atthill, *Old Mendip*, David and Charles 1964, p. 172.
6 Joseph Priestley, p. 614.
7 H. R. de Salis, *Handbook*, p. 359.
8 Charles Hadfield, *Canals of Southern England*, p. 229.
9 E. T. MacDermot, *History of the Great Western Railway*, G.W.R. 1931, vol. 2, p. 167.
10 *Ibid*.
11 *Ibid*, p. 166.
12 H. R. de Salis, *Chronology of Inland Navigation*, p. 164.
13 *Ibid*, p. 73.
14 Joseph Priestley, p. 112.

CHAPTER NINE

1 For a full account of Hawkesbury Pumping Station and its engines see C. T. G. Boucher, 'The pumping station at Hawkesbury Junction', Newcomen Society *Transactions*, vol. 35, 1962–63.
2 Information from Mr B. W. Carter, Cirencester.
3 Information from Mr C. M. Marsh, British Waterways, Northwich.
4 Joseph Priestley, p. 420.
5 For a description of canal lifts in the U.S. and Europe, see D. H. Tew, 'Canal lifts and inclines', Newcomen Society *Transactions*, vol. 28, 1951–53.

6 William Chapman, *Observations on the Various Systems of Canal Navigation*, 1797.

7 *Ibid.*

8 *Ibid.*

9 Charles Hadfield, *Canals of the West Midlands*.

10 *Ibid.*

11 Thomas Telford, writing in *Plymley's Shropshire*, 1797.

12 H. R. de Salis, *Handbook*, p. 217.

13 William Chapman.

14 Robert Fulton, *A Treatise on Canal Navigation*, 1796.

15 D. H. Tew.

16 *Ibid.*

17 Telford Papers, Institution of Civil Engineers Library.

18 Charles Hadfield, *Canals of South Wales and the Border*, p. 40.

19 D. H. Tew.

20 Charles Hadfield, *Canals of the East Midlands*, p. 227.

21 Anderson, *General View of the Agriculture and Rural Economy of the County of Aberdeen*, 1794.

22 Robert Fulton, *Treatise*, Plate 11.

23 Charles Hadfield, *Canals of the East Midlands*, p. 130.

24 Original drawing reproduced by Charles Hadfield, *Canals of Southern England*, p. 153.

25 William Chapman.

26 Telford Papers, I.C.E. Library.

27 Charles Hadfield, *Canals of the East Midlands*, p. 36.

28 D. H. Tew.

29 *Ibid.*

CHAPTER TEN

1 Institution of Civil Engineers, *Proceedings*, vol. 15, 1856, p. 198.

2 Kelly's *Directory of Gloucestershire*, 1935 edn.

3 Margaret Dickins, *A Thousand Years in Tardebigge* Cornish 1931, p. 101.

4 Joseph Priestley, p. 334.

5 H. G. W. Household, 'Early Engineering on the Thames & Severn Canal', Newcomen Society, *Transactions* vol. 27, 1949–1951.

6 Information from H. Ballinger, Gloucester, who worked through the canal as a youth with his father.

7 Joseph Priestley, p. 592.

8 H. Philip Spratt, *The Birth of the Steam Boat*, Griffin 1958, p. 57.

9 *Ibid.*

10 H. Malet, *The Canal Duke*, p. 157.

11 *Ibid.*

12 L. T. C. Rolt, *Thomas Newcomen*, David and Charles 1963, p. 132.

13 H. Malet.

14 H. P. Spratt.

15 *Ibid.*

16 G. K. Scott, *Matthew Murray, Pioneer Engineer*, 1928, p. 14.

17 Charles Hadfield, *Canals of the East Midlands*, p. 76.

18 Charles Hadfield, *Canals of the West Midlands*, p. 118.

19 *Ibid*, p. 212.

20 Information on Leeds & Liverpool Steamers supplied by Mr Gordon Roberts.

21 For illustration of an L. & L. steamer at work, see Rolt, *Inland Waterways of England*, Plate 38.

22 Information on Fellows, Morton and Clayton steamers supplied by C. N. Hadlow, Curator, Waterways Museum, Stoke Bruerne.

Gazetteer

*Objects of outstanding interest on the waterways
(nearest classified road indicated in brackets)*

MUSEUM

The Waterways Museum, Stoke Bruerne, near Towcester. This is
the official Museum of British Waterways, appropriately housed in a
warehouse in one of the prettiest canal-side villages close to A508
and midway between the A5 and the M1. A fascinating collection of
prints, photographs and three dimensional objects ranging up to a
full-sized replica of a narrow boat cabin, furnished in the traditional
style. Information from: The Curator, Waterways Museum, Stoke
Bruerne, near Towcester, Northants. Telephone: Roade 229.

AQUEDUCTS (MASONRY)

Lune. Lancaster Canal, river Lune (Rennie), undoubtedly the
finest masonry aqueduct in the country. Near Lancaster (A683).

Marple. Peak Forest Canal, river Mersey (Outram). An impressive
structure with pierced spandrels, 90 ft high. Recently restored.
(A628).

Lea Wood. Cromford Canal, river Derwent (Jessop). A single arch
structure with unusually large span of 80 ft. Lea Wood Pumping
Station adjoins (*q.v.*). Also see terminal buildings of Cromford
& High Peak Tramway. Cromford (A6).

Dove. Trent & Mersey Canal, river Dove (Brindley). With twenty-
three arches this is the largest example surviving of a Brindley
aqueduct. Near Burton-on-Trent (A38).

Chirk. Ellesmere Canal, river Ceiriog (Telford). Splendid multispan structure with iron base 70 ft high crossing the Welsh border.
See also Chirk Tunnel with towpath. Chirk (A5).

Dundas and *Avoncliff.* Kennet & Avon Canal, River Avon, (Rennie).
Outstanding examples of Rennie's monumental style in Bath
stone. Near Limpley Stoke (A36).

AQUEDUCTS (IRON TROUGH)

Longdon-upon-Tern. Shrewsbury Canal, River Tern (Telford/
Clowes/Reynolds) the first large iron trough aqueduct. Longdon
(B5063).

Pont Cysyllte. Ellesmere Canal, River Dee (Telford/Hazledine).
Undoubtedly the most remarkable work of canal engineering in
the British Isles. 127 ft high. Carries canal across Vale of Llangollen. Inscription on pier immediately south of river. Also southern
approach embankment (*q.v.*). Vron Cysyllte (A5) or Trevor
(A539).

Edstone. Stratford-on-Avon Canal (James). After Pont Cysyllte, the
longest iron trough aqueduct in the country, carrying the canal at
no great height across the valley of the Edstone brook in which
two railways were built subsequently. Near Bearley (A34). See
also smaller iron trough aqueduct over A34 at Wootton Wawen.

TUNNELS

Harecastle. Trent & Mersey Canal. Two tunnels, Old (Brindley)
2,897 yds, the first major canal tunnel in the country now disused,
and New (Telford) 2,926 yds with towing path which is now impassable. The two make a good contrasting example of 'first and
last' in canal engineering. Kidsgrove (A50).

Standedge. Huddersfield Narrow Canal, under Standedge Fell,
Pennines (Outram/Clowes/Rooth). At 5,456 yds, this is by far the
longest canal tunnel in the country and stands on the highest
summit level, 656 ft. No towing path and disused, but organized
parties are occasionally taken through by boat. Diggle (W. end)
Marsden (E. end) (A62).

Blisworth. Grand Junction Canal (Jessop/Barnes) 3,056 yds. The
longest canal tunnel still in regular use. The S. end of the tunnel
is close to the Waterways Museum (*q.v.*). For N. end, Blisworth
(A43).

Sapperton. Thames & Severn Canal (Whitworth) 3,808 yds, the
second longest canal tunnel in the country carrying canal under
the Cotswold scarp. Tunnel House Inn by classical N. portal. S
portal romantically situated at head of Golden Valley. Interior
blocked by roof falls. Sapperton (W. end), Coate (E. end) (A419)

Dudley. Dudley Canal (Dadford/Clowes) 3,172 yds. An early 'leg-ging' tunnel with remarkable series of limestone caverns near N. end. Disused, but efforts are being made to preserve and parties are occasionally taken through by boat. Near Dudley (A6).

Netherton. Birmingham Canal Navigations (??) 3,027 yds. Built 1855–58 to relieve Dudley tunnel, this was the last canal tunnel to be built in England. Two towpaths; originally lit by gas and later by electric light. Near Dudley (A6).

LOCKS AND LIFTS

Tardebigge. Worcester & Birmingham Canal (Woodhouse). Flight of thirty narrow locks, best seen from dam of Tardebigge Reservoir. Unusually deep top lock replaces lift. Top of flight: Tardebigge (A448). See also Tardebigge canal workshops and tunnel.

Devizes. Kennet & Avon Canal (Rennie) spectacula flight of twenty-nine broad locks with ponds terraced in the hillside. Devizes (A361).

Bingley Five Rise. Leeds & Liverpool Canal (Longbotham). An impressive staircase of five broad locks. Bingley (A650).

Foxton. Grand Union Canal (Bevan). Two staircases, each of five narrow locks. See also remains of Foxton Inclined Plane Lift. Foxton, near Market Harborough (A6).

Bratch. Staffordshire & Worcestershire Canal (Brindley/Dadford). Unique flight of three narrow locks with miniscule intermediate pounds supplied by side ponds beyond towpath. Near Wombourne (A449). See also Botterham double lock, south of Wombourne.

Neptune's Staircase. Caledonian Canal (Telford). Flight of eight ship canal locks in superb surroundings. Banavie, near Fort William (A830). See also Laggan summit cutting, near Invergarry (A82).

Anderton Lift. Trent & Mersey Canal/River Weaver. (Williams/ Clark). The only canal lift in the country still operating. Two caissons lower boats 50 ft vertically down to river from canal. Originally hydraulic, now electric. Anderton, near Northwich (A533). See also canal tunnels at Barnton, Saltersford and Preston Brook.

CANAL PUMPING STATIONS

Lea Wood. Cromford Canal. Original stone pump house with single beam engine. Can be inspected by arrangement. Near the Lea Wood aqueduct (*q.v.*). Cromford (A6).

Crofton. Kennet & Avon Canal. Original brick pump-house housing two beam engines, one original Boulton and Watt, the second a Cornish engine by Harveys. Can be inspected by arrangement. Working until recently. Near Great Bedwyn (A4 or A338).

Claverton. Kennet & Avon Canal. Unique installation of beam pumps driven through gearing by undershot waterwheels driven by leat off river Avon. Can be inspected by arrangement. Claverton, near Bath (A36).

EARTHWORKS

Stretford and *Bollin* embankments. Bridgewater Canal (Brindley/ Morris). The first substantial earthworks of their kind ever raised. For Stretford, Barton near Eccles (A57). For Bollin, Bollington near Altrincham (A56). At Barton, see also the remarkable swing aqueduct (Leader Williams) which replaced the original Barton aqueduct when the Manchester Ship Canal was built.

Burnley. Leeds & Liverpool Canal. (Whitworth). A great curving embankment affording magnificent prospect over industrial Burnley (A56).

Smethwick. Birmingham Canal, deep cutting by Telford dominated by his fine cast-iron Galton Bridge. Part of the 1828–39 improvement scheme. Near Birmingham.

Pont Cysyllte, the southern approach embankment, Ellesmere Canal. (Telford). Reaching a height of 97 ft at tip, this, at the time of completion, was the greatest earthwork ever raised. Owing to the proximity of the aqueduct and the fact that the embankment is tree-covered, it tends to be ignored. Vron Cysyllte (A5).

Shelmore Bank and *Grub Street Cutting*. Birmingham & Liverpool Junction Canal (Telford). Typical of the heavy earthworks on this last trunk line of canal. Shelmore gave so much trouble that Telford died before it was completed. Norbury, near Newport, Salop (A519). See also Knighton Bank, N. of Grub Street and Woodseaves Cutting near Market Drayton (A529) on the same canal.

TOW PATHS

Towpath walking is the next best thing to travelling by boat. Any towpath makes a worthwhile walk, but the following are specially recommended.

Brecon & Abergavenny Canal. Pontymoile–Brecon, thirty-three miles. Superb scenery overlooking the valley of the Usk. Magnificent trees, particularly on section bordering Glanusk Park. Canal features: Llanfoist wharf and remains of old tramways; Llangynidr locks; Aqueducts at Gilwern and Brynich; Ashford tunnel, near Talybont.

Ellesmere Canal (1). Hampton Bank (B5063 crosses) to Ellesmere, four miles. Delightful walk through the Shropshire lake district. Canal skirts Cole Mere and Blake Mere. Canal features: old lime kilns at Hampton Bank; short Ellesmere tunnel (87 yds) with towpath; Ellesmere Canal Depot and Beech House, the latter built by Telford and once the headquarters of the Canal Company.

Ellesmere Canal (2). Chirk Bank (A5) to Llantisilio, ten miles. One of the most sensational walks in Britain, with views of the Vales of Ceiriog and Llangollen. Canal features: Chirk and Pont Cysyllte aqueducts, Chirk (459 yds) and Whitehouses (191 yds) tunnels with towpath through (a torch is advisable in the former), old basin and boatyard at Pont Cysyllte north end, intake at Horseshoe Falls.

Kennet & Avon Canal. Bradford-on-Avon to junction with R. Avon at Bath, ten miles. Romantic views of the Avon Valley and Bath. Canal features: Avoncliff and Dundas aqueducts, Claverton Pumping Station, fine architectural 'landscaping' by Rennie at Sydney Gardens, Bath.

Select Bibliography

The following books are recommended for further reading. They are all either currently in print or so recent that they should be readily available from a Public Library.

GENERAL

de Maré, Eric. *The Canals of England*, Architectural Press, 1950. Notable for Mr de Maré's superb photographs.

Edwards, L. A. *The Inland Waterways of Great Britain and Ireland*, Imray 1962. Tabulated and factual information for voyagers covering the waterways of England, Wales, Scotland and N. Ireland. The modern equivalent of de Salis's *Handbook* (Bradshaw) which is difficult to obtain and covers only England and Wales.

Hadfield, C. *British Canals*, 2nd edn. David and Charles, 1962. A general history.

——*Introducing Canals*, Benn, 1955. A very useful and comprehensive beginner's guide to the subject.

Rolt, L. T. C. *Inland Waterways of England*. Allen and Unwin, 1950. Features of the waterways, their operation and the customs and working methods of the canal boatmen.

Willan, T. S. *River Navigation in England 1600–1750*, 2nd edn. Cass, 1964. Oxford U.P. A standard work. Published in 1936, but still the only authoritative historical study of the early River Navigations.

REGIONAL

Hadfield, C. *The Canals of South-West England*, 1967, *The Canals of South Wales and The Border*, 1960, *The Canals of the East Midlands*, 1966, *The Canals of the West Midlands*, 1966.

McCutcheon, W. A. *The Canals of the North of Ireland*, 1965.

Delany, V. T. H. and Delany, D. R. *The Canals of the South of Ireland*, 1966.

Lindsay, Jean. *The Canals of Scotland*, 1968.

This series of regional canal histories, all published by David and Charles, makes a most valuable contribution to our knowledge of waterway history and is thoroughly recommended as a reliable source of historical information. *The Canals of South-West England* supersedes *The Canals of Southern England* which is referred to in this book and the canals of south-east England will be dealt with in a separate volume.

LOCAL

Clew, Kenneth. *The Kennet & Avon Canal*, David and Charles, 1968.

Hadfield, C. and Norris, J. *Waterways to Stratford*, David and Charles, 1962, The Upper Avon Navigation, the Stratford Canal and the Stratford & Moreton Tramway.

Tew, David. *The Oakham Canal*, Brewhouse Press, 1967.

Vine, P. A. L. *London's Lost Route to the Sea*, David and Charles, 1965. A fascinating study with many rare illustrations of the Wey & Arun Canal and its associated waterways. Strongly recommended.

——*London's Lost Route to Basingstoke*, David and Charles, 1968. A companion volume to the above on the history of the Basingstoke Canal.

Wilkinson, T. *Hold on a Minute*, Allen and Unwin, 1965. An autobiographical account of commercial narrow boating on the Grand Union Canal. A good picture of the life of the working boatmen on the G.U.C. in the recent past.

BIOGRAPHY

Boucher, Cyril T. G. *John Rennie*, Manchester U.P. 1963. The only modern biography of Rennie and a valuable assessment of his achievement as an engineer.

Malet, Hugh. *The Canal Duke*, David and Charles, 1961. A modern biography of Francis, third Duke of Bridgewater which makes use of original sources and sheds valuable new light, not only on the Duke, but on James Brindley.

Rolt, L. T. C. *Thomas Telford*, Longmans, 1958. A modern biography of Telford with chapters devoted to the building of the Ellesmere, Caledonian, Gotha and Birmingham & Liverpool Junction canals.

CANAL TRAMWAYS

Baxter, Bertram. *Stone Blocks and Iron Rails*, David and Charles, 1966. The results of a lifetime of study and fieldwork. Includes a Gazetteer covering all known tramways in England, Wales and Scotland. Consult it for further information on all the canal tramways mentioned in this book.

MAP

Stanford's *Inland Cruising Map of England* is recommended. All locks and tunnels are marked.

Index